FINDING
THE
NEW TESTAMENT

An Introductory Course on

New Testament Textual Criticism

FINDING
THE
NEW TESTAMENT

An Introductory Course on

New Testament Textual Criticism

Second Edition

Graham Simpson

SAIACS Press

Bangalore, India

2018

Finding the New Testament

An Introductory Course in New Testament Textual Criticism

Second Edition

Copyright © Graham Simpson 2018

ISBN: 978-93-86549-09-9

Published by SAIACS Press

SAIACS
P.O. Box 7747, Kothanur, Bangalore 560 077, India
saiacspress@saiacs.org
www.saiacs.org

Layout: Graham Simpson
Cover Design: Ashley Roberts

Printed by SAIACS Printing Services, Bangalore
printservices@saiacs.org

To Heather

for loving support and unfailing encouragement
over nearly half a century together

CONTENTS

PART I: THE HISTORY AND THEORY OF TEXTUAL CRITICISM

PART II: THE PRACTICE OF TEXTUAL CRITICISM

PART III: FOR REFLECTION

APPENDICES

PREFACE

I make no claim to be a professional expert in this area. I stand in awe of those who have written some of the standard textbooks, who have done detailed study of the manuscripts, and who have edited Greek New Testaments. However, textual criticism is a subject in which I have taken an interest for a long time and I am happy to regard myself as an enthusiastic amateur with better than average knowledge of the subject. I bought my first Greek New Testament (the blue-covered British and Foreign Bible Society edition) soon after I started learning Greek at school in 1961. From the start I was fascinated by the strange notes that appeared at the foot of each page. It is those notes that contain the significant variants contained in the New Testament manuscripts, which provide the basic material for textual criticism. Over the years I have become more familiar with all this, and in the last decade or so have had the privilege of teaching textual criticism a number of times to postgraduate students in India.

It is my hope that the publication of this book may lead to the subject being taught more frequently in theological institutions in India and elsewhere, especially at MTh level, and possibly also for BD and MDiv students doing biblical studies at an advanced level. There are other and no doubt bigger and better books, but they are usually not written specifically to be used as a course textbook, and certainly not readily available at an affordable price in India. At the same time this book is not intended to compete with the well-established textbooks. On the contrary, students are encouraged to see this book as a starting point and to expand their knowledge from other resources. You will find many suggestions for further reading.

Potential teachers may be interested to know how I approach the subject. In an intensive module of three or four weeks, I deal with chapter 1 and chapters 7-12 in the first week, which gets students looking at the textual apparatus fairly soon and provides some necessary tools. In that same week students are given the assignment of reading chapters 2-6 (which are necessary historical background) and preparing answers to the questions at the end of each of these chapters. In the second week they give their answers in the form of class presentations, and opportunity is also taken in that week to revise and practise material introduced in the first week. By the third week, after dealing with chapter 13 the class is ready to start doing actual textual criticism, focussing on the examples discussed in chapters 14, 15 and 16. Many or few of these examples can be studied, according to the time available; it is certainly not necessary to look at them all. If a fourth week is available, there is an unlimited pool of other examples to work on, and chapter 17 provides some suggestions. Chapter 18 and appendix 5 introduce some of the theological implications raised by textual criticism. Some samples of textual criticism are required to be submitted as a written assignment, and there is a final examination. The experienced teacher will, of course, work out their own preferred approach, and much will depend on the specifics of their own seminary's context.

Production of a second edition has made it possible to correct a number of typographical mistakes as well as some other errors of detail. Some material has been rewritten in order to improve the clarity of expression, and occasionally there is an extra sentence or paragraph. However, there is no substantial change from the first edition.

It is a delight to dedicate this book to my wife Heather, to whom I owe more than can ever be expressed. I also want to acknowledge a great debt of gratitude to Dr Cornelis Bennema, my former colleague at the South Asia Institute of Advanced Christian Studies (Bangalore, India), who realised the fundamental importance of textual criticism for New Testament studies and did everything in his power to see that it was included in the curriculum.

INTRODUCTION

If you are totally unfamiliar with the subject of textual criticism, you may be curious about the title *Finding the New Testament*. You may wonder, "What needs to be found?" You can easily find it on the shelf of any Christian bookshop, and that is good enough for most Christians.

The aim of textual criticism, as it has been traditionally understood, is to identify the actual words which the writer of any particular New Testament book originally wrote, or, if in some cases we cannot be sure of the original words, the closest we can get to that goal. Some scholars in recent times have challenged this traditional view, but we will accept this definition for this course.

We regularly use our New Testament with an acceptance of the particular text we are reading, whether Greek, English or our vernacular language, with little or no thought about the originality or reliability of the text. Probably most Bible readers ignore the notes which appear at the foot of the page (in most modern English translations, at least). Many of the notes are about translation issues, offering alternative translations, or a more literal translation than in the text. But for our present purpose the notes of greatest interest are the ones about the actual text, usually beginning "other ancient authorities read ... " or "other ancient authorities add ... " or "other ancient authorities lack ... " These *ancient authorities* are Greek manuscripts or other sources where early forms of the New Testament text have been preserved, which provide evidence of differences in the words of the text. Where such differences occur, which version is the original? Who decides? On what basis?

There is a lot of evidence, from thousands of Greek manuscripts, early translations into other ancient languages, and quotations in early Christian writers (the Fathers). The challenge is what to do with all this evidence. No manuscript can be claimed to be the original of the NT or of any particular book of the NT, and so we have thousands of documents and other pieces of evidence which provide *indirect* evidence of the text of the NT. The question is how we use all this evidence to recover the original text. It has been claimed that with so much evidence the original words of any particular NT verse must have survived somewhere. This is a reasonable claim but it cannot be proved, and it is possible that in a given passage the original has *not* been preserved in any source. But, assuming that this claim is correct in nearly every situation where a variant occurs, how can we identify the original words and distinguish them from the large number of changes which have arisen in the process of copying manuscripts? There is indeed a New Testament to be found, among the many variants which have come down to us.

This is the subject matter of this course. It is assumed that the reader has a basic knowledge of Greek and will use this book in conjunction with the Greek New Testament text contained in the United Bible Societies 5th edition (UBS⁵). For the benefit of the student who is using the 4th edition (UBS⁴), we will note any relevant differences in the appropriate places. UBS⁴ itself was reprinted many times and the introductory material in particular is not the same in each printing. The page numbers for UBS⁴ given in this book are from the 13th printing of 2007.

Note the abbreviations listed on page 147 for other books which are frequently referred to, as well as the abbreviations MS (manuscript) and MSS (manuscripts).

PART I

THE HISTORY AND THEORY OF
TEXTUAL CRITICISM

Chapter 1

WHAT DOES IT MATTER?

As a preliminary exercise, copy any two paragraphs from the introduction in your own handwriting on to a separate sheet of paper.

We want to know, as accurately as possible, what were the original words of each NT document. The basic problem is that the books of the NT were produced long before the invention of the printing press. When a book is published today, we can expect that all copies will be the same. The copy sold in Delhi will be exactly the same as a copy of the same book sold in Chennai. But in earlier centuries the only way to reproduce a book was through copying by hand, thus requiring the work of scribes. A printing press is a machine; it may break down and need repair, but it does not think and it does not make changes in the text that is being printed. An ancient scribe was very capable of making changes, sometimes *accidentally* perhaps because he was tired and not concentrating properly and so he misread a word or his eye returned to the wrong place in the MS from which he was copying (called the exemplar). Sometimes he thought that his exemplar was wrong (that is, that an earlier scribe had made a mistake), and so he *deliberately* changed the text, perhaps to improve the grammar or to remove what he considered to be an error of theology or historical fact. In one way or another changes were inevitably made by scribes while copying texts. If you have done the exercise given at the beginning of this chapter, look at your own scribal work, or preferably ask someone else to look at it. How many changes have you made from the original? Changes (deliberate or accidental) are inevitable, and so the need for textual criticism arose the first time a NT book was copied. During fifteen centuries of copying (before the invention of the printing press) many thousands of changes have come into the text. It has been recently estimated by P. Gurry (*NTStud* 62 (2016), 97-121) that there are about 500,000 variants. Here is the simple answer to the question in the chapter heading. If we want to find the original text of the NT, textual criticism is necessary.

In order to do textual criticism we need access to the evidence, the possible variants for a given passage. Some of these are given in the footnotes of standard editions of the Greek New Testament, such as the United Bible Societies' text (5th edition, 2014, or 4th edition, 1993) and the Nestle-Aland text (28th edition, 2012), with the appropriate evidence in support of each variant. Fortunately for us who are tackling textual criticism at an amateur level, we do not need *all* the variants (many of which are quite trivial anyway). If all of them were given, the UBS[5] edition, which has 856 pages, would need to print about 580 variants on each page; in fact each page has only two or three (six on one page [339], five on eight pages [213, 453, 771, 774, 779, 781, 795, 817], four on 39 pages), with many pages containing one or even no textual note. The NA[28] edition of 789 pages contains a larger number of variants (roughly 20 per page) but it would need to print over 630 variants on each page to cover all 500,000. This means that the experts have already done a lot of the preliminary ground-clearing work and have provided in the footnotes of the commonly used editions of the Greek NT a convenient collection of variants which we need to consider. These footnotes are called the apparatus or critical apparatus or in Latin *apparatus criticus*. So here is our task. What do these footnotes mean? How can we interpret them? How can we use them to decide what is the original text of the NT?

There are two major periods in the story of the NT text. First are the fifteen centuries during which MSS were copied by hand, one at a time. During this long period the variants (changes in the text) arose which make textual criticism necessary. So this period provides us with the resources, the raw material, for textual criticism. By the end of this course you should have developed some skill in evaluating the variants and will be able to do some basic textual criticism.

But it is difficult (in fact almost impossible) to practise textual criticism unless we first understand what happened in the second major period, from the sixteenth century till now. This period tells the history of textual criticism, that is, what previous generations of scholars have done with the variants which they have discovered in the witnesses to the NT text. During this period different approaches have been tried, and from these have developed the techniques of modern textual criticism. We cannot use the modern techniques unless we understand the story, identifying the main stages and the principles of textual criticism which have been developed as the story has unfolded. The story of textual criticism can be summed up as a quest for answers to two main questions: First, what happened to the NT text during the first fifteen centuries? The challenge here is to understand the history of the development of the text. Second, how do we evaluate the many variants in an orderly way? The challenge here is to attempt to reconstruct the actual text of the NT.

Two further preliminary points may be made, perhaps a necessary reassurance to some students. First, textual criticism (that is, a critical study of the wording of the text of the NT documents) is not a negative discipline but essentially a positive enterprise, an attempt to discover the exact words of the text as written by the original authors. Don't be concerned by the word *criticism*.

Second, the observation that there may be 500,000 variants within the NT MSS should not cause any alarm. If our copy of the NT contains about 300 pages, that means more than 1,500 points of uncertainty on each page, which may seem a staggeringly large number, and may lead some to think that we really have little idea what the NT actually says. But that would be an unnecessarily pessimistic conclusion and it is worth taking a few moments to identify the nature of the variants. We will take John 16 as an example, using the information provided in the NA²⁸ edition (the UBS editions do not record as many variants, for reasons which we will see later). We need to remember that thousands of trivial variants (minor spelling mistakes, for example) have already been excluded from consideration.

Many variants in John 16 are of little consequence. In these examples the variant does not even need a different English translation:

Verse	Text as printed	Variant in apparatus	Description of the difference
7	μὴ ἀπέλθω	ἐγὼ μὴ ἀπέλθω	Addition of ἐγώ
19	ὁ Ἰησοῦς	Ἰησοῦς	Omission of article ὁ
19	ἐρωτᾶν	ἐρωτῆσαι	Present or aorist infinitive
20	ὑμεῖς	ὑμεῖς δέ	Addition of δέ
22	αἴρει	ἀφαίρει	Simple or compound verb
24	αἰτεῖτε	αἰτήσασθε	Present active or aorist middle imperative
27	τοῦ θεοῦ	θεοῦ	Omission of article τοῦ
29	ἐν παρρησίᾳ	παρρησίᾳ	Omission of preposition ἐν
31	Ἰησοῦς	ὁ Ἰησοῦς	Addition of article ὁ
33	ταῦτα	ταῦτα δέ	Addition of δέ

Other variants in John 16 do change the translation but may also be considered of minor importance:

Verse	Text as printed	Variant in apparatus	Description of the difference
2	ὁ ἀποκτείνας ὑμᾶς	ὁ ἀποκτείνας	Omission of object *you* after *kill*
7	οὐκ ἐλεύσεται	οὐ μὴ ἔλθῃ	Future tense or emphatic future
13	ὁδηγήσει	διηγήσεται	Different words with similar meaning
15	εἶπον	εἶπον ὑμῖν	Addition of *to you*
16	οὐκέτι	οὐ	*No longer* or *not*
17	οὐ	οὐκέτι	*Not* or *no longer*
19	οὐ	οὐκέτι	*Not* or *no longer*
21	ὥρα	ἡμέρα	Different words with similar meaning
21	θλίψεως	λύπης	Different words with similar meaning
22	ἔχετε	ἔξετε	Present or future
23	ἄν τι αἰτήσητε	ὃ ἂν αἰτήσητε	*If you ask anything* or *whatever you ask*
25	ἀπαγγελῶ	ἀπαγγέλλω	Future or present
28	παρά	ἐκ	Different words with similar meaning
29	λέγουσιν	λέγουσιν αὐτῷ	Addition of *to him*
32	σκορπισθῆτε	σκορπισθῆτε πάντες	Addition of *all* with the subject *you*
33	ἔχετε	ἔξετε	Present or future

But these other variants in John 16 seem to be quite significant:

Verse	Variant	Description of the difference
1	Omission of μή	*In order that you may not fall away* or *in order that you may fall away*
3	Omission of the whole verse	
7	Omission of ἐὰν δὲ πορευθῶ, πέμψω αὐτὸν πρὸς ὑμᾶς	Omission of *If I go, I will send him to you*

15	Omission of the whole verse	
16	Addition of ὅτι ὑπάγω πρὸς τὸν πατέρα	Addition of *Because I am going to the Father*
33	Omission of ἐν τῷ κόσμῳ θλῖψιν ἔχετε	Omission of *In the world you have affliction*

Here is a list of variants from Colossians 2:6-23. Try to give your own opinion whether the passage represents a significant or a relatively insignificant variation. Does the variation represent a change in the meaning of the text, or simply a change which makes little or no difference to the meaning? Describe the variation in any way you think is relevant, perhaps using the preceding tables as a guide. At this stage we are not attempting to evaluate the relative merits of the variants but only to get a taste of the type of variation which is to be found in the NT MSS.

Verse	Text as printed	Variant(s) given in the apparatus
7	τῇ πίστει	ἐν πίστει *or* ἐν τῇ πίστει
7	ἐν εὐχαριστίᾳ	ἐν αὐτῇ ἐν εὐχαριστίᾳ *or* ἐν αὐτῇ *or* ἐν αὐτῷ ἐν εὐχαριστίᾳ
11	τοῦ σώματος τῆς σαρκός	τοῦ σώματος τῶν ἁμαρτιῶν τῆς σαρκός
12	ἐν τῷ βαπτισμῷ	ἐν τῷ βαπτίσματι
12	ἐκ νεκρῶν	ἐκ τῶν νεκρῶν
13	ὑμᾶς	ἡμᾶς
13	ἡμῖν	ὑμῖν
14	τοῖς δόγμασιν	Words omitted
19	τὴν κεφαλήν	τὴν κεφαλὴν Χριστόν
20	εἰ ἀπεθάνετε	εἰ οὖν ἀπεθάνετε
23	ταπεινοφροσύνῃ	ταπεινοφροσύνῃ τοῦ νοός
23	καὶ ἀφειδίᾳ σώματος	καί omitted

As a further reassurance, it can be said that even where there is a *significant* variant (that is, a variant which may affect the translation and exegesis of the passage in a significant way), it is often not difficult for a textual critic to explain why one of the options can be confidently identified as the earliest. After you have completed this course, you will be able to do this yourself.

However, the task remains. Whether a variant is considered significant or insignificant, and whether or not it is fairly straightforward to identify the earliest reading out of the available variants, it is necessary in any case to go through the text-critical processes in order to come to a defensible view of the earliest possible form of the text of the Greek NT.

That is what we will do eventually. But first we need to look at the story of textual criticism, from the first printed editions of the Greek NT until the present.

Revision Questions

1   Explain what textual criticism is and why it is a necessary aspect of NT studies.
2   What is the obvious dividing point in the story of the NT text? Briefly state what happened up to that point and what has happened since then.
3   What is your own reaction to the types of variants which we find in the MSS of the NT?

Chapter 2

FROM MANUSCRIPT TO PRINTED TEXT

As we know, the NT text has been reproduced during most of its history through the hand-produced copying of MSS one by one. We will look later at the work of the scribes and the results of scribal changes introduced accidentally or deliberately into the text (chapter 7). We will not go into detail about the actual process of the production, publication and copying of NT books in MS form, but P. Comfort has a useful chapter on this topic (chapter 1, "The Manuscript Publications of the Greek New Testament", pages 1-54), if you would like more information about this.

The invention of printing in the 15th century changed the situation entirely regarding the production of the NT text. No longer were copies of the NT produced one by one, each one being inevitably different from all the others, but now it became possible to produce thousands of identical copies. The commercial advantages in this new situation are obvious, and it is no surprise that there was a rush to be the first to publish the New Testament in Greek. The first copies to come on to the market were the first edition of the text edited by Erasmus of Rotterdam in 1516. Four other editions of Erasmus followed.

In spite of Erasmus' reputation as a scholar, it was commercial benefit rather than scholarship which seemed to be his main motivation. The fact that scholarship was not the main consideration in the production of this edition is illustrated by the following:

1   The text of the first edition was based on a few late MSS from the twelfth and thirteenth centuries, with several others used for purposes of comparison. The earliest and best MS available to him was from the tenth century (codex 1), but this he used *least* because of his opinion that its text was unreliable.

2   He had only one MS containing the text of Revelation, of which the last page with the last six verses of the book was missing. Erasmus solved this problem very simply by making his own translation from the Latin into the Greek, thus creating some readings not found in any Greek MS.

3   In 1 John 5:7-8 Erasmus in his first edition omitted the trinitarian statement which was in the Vulgate (the statement about "the Father,

the Word and the Holy Spirit ... ", which is found in the KJV but not
in most modern English translations). In response to criticism he said
that he had not found the passage in any Greek MS available to him,
but foolishly promised to include it if such a MS were found. Such a
MS *was* found, and so Erasmus included the words in his 1522 edition.
It was discovered later that this was not a genuine ancient MS but had
been specially produced about 1520 in order to meet this specific
need!

Erasmus' text became the standard which was followed in other printed
editions. As a result it was also the text used as the basis of all translations
in the following centuries, including the famous 1611 English translation
(the Authorised Version or King James Version). One of the many Greek
editions based on Erasmus' text was a 1633 edition produced by the
Elzevir brothers, in which they claimed: "Therefore you now have the text
received by all." This was merely publishers' propaganda, but from this
claim has come the phrase "received text" (in its Latin form *textus receptus*
and commonly referred to by the abbreviation TR). All the Greek New
Testaments printed till that time (approximately 160 editions) used much
the same text, and so it was indeed the "text received by all".

By the time of the Elzevirs the TR was already well established and it
continued to be unchallenged for another 250 years (till the end of the
nineteenth century). But during this period much scholarly work was
being done on the NT text, both in the collection of evidence and in
thinking about how the evidence should be used.

It is neither possible nor necessary to give a full survey of this long period,
but it will be useful to mention some of the important names and to
summarise their work. Of special importance was J.A. Bengel (1687-1752),
who formulated the principle that witnesses must not be counted but
weighed, classified in "companies, families, tribes, nations". He distinguished two major groups: (a) Asiatic, originating from Constantinople
(MSS of more recent date), and (b) African, with two subdivisions
represented by codex Alexandrinus and the Old Latin version. He stated
the principle of preference for the harder reading to the easier. His printed
edition followed the TR but with marginal notes indicating: α the original
reading, β a better reading than that printed, γ a reading as good as that
printed, δ an inferior reading to that printed, ε a very inferior reading.

Somewhat later J.J. Griesbach (1745-1812) gave special attention to patristic
quotations and to previously little-studied versions (eg Gothic, Armenian,
Philoxenian Syriac). He further developed a picture of the grouping of
MSS, resulting in three groups:

1   Alexandrian (C, L, K; 1, 13, 33, 69, 106, 118; Bohairic, Armenian, Ethiopic, Harclean Syriac; Origen, Clement of Alexandria, Eusebius, Cyril of Alexandria, Isidore of Pelusium).
2   Western (D; Latin, Peshitta Syriac [part], Arabic [part]).
3   Byzantine, a later compilation from the other two (A [Gospels]; most later uncials and minuscules; most patristic quotations).

Griesbach's edition significantly differed from the TR, though the TR continued in common use.

Significant scholars in the nineteenth century include K. Lachmann (1793-1851), C. von Tischendorf (1815-1874) and S.P. Tregelles (1813-1875). Lachmann rejected the TR, and using scientific methods of textual criticism, he printed a text which he claimed to represent the text current at Constantinople about AD 380, though it was based on only a handful of MSS (seldom more than four and in some sections only one). Tischendorf produced eight editions of the Greek NT and 22 volumes of texts of biblical MSS. His main contribution lay in the collecting of textual evidence, including the discovery of significant MSS such as codex Sinaiticus at St Catherine's Monastery on Mount Sinai. His actual editions show a lack of consistency in applying textual principles, the last displaying an overemphasis on Sinaiticus which he had recently discovered. British scholars had also been active over this period of several centuries. One of them, Tregelles, made a careful study of many of the then-known uncials and of some important minuscules, and corrected previous errors in the citation of evidence. He also made a fresh examination of patristic citations and versions. He also produced a Greek NT edition as the end result of his scholarly labours.

In these ways scholars had begun to realise the weaknesses of the Textus Receptus. We can summarise developments to this stage as follows:

1   Many variant readings were collected (ie variations from the TR).
2   Principles of textual criticism were being formulated, ie criteria by which the variants could be assessed.
3   Earlier MSS were being discovered and studied.
4   MS groups were being identified, of which the Byzantine text was regarded as only one and indeed the latest of them all.
5   New editions of the Greek NT began to be published, with significant differences from the TR.

For the material of this chapter, see further *Textual Commentary*, 7*-10*; Metzger & Ehrman, 137-174; Aland, 3-14; Comfort, 97-99; E.J. Epp in Epp & Fee, chapter 2.

Revision Questions

1   What was the significance of Erasmus in the story of the text of the
     NT, both short-term and long-term?
2   In what ways can Erasmus be considered both a success and a
     failure?
3   What is meant by the phrase *Textus Receptus*? What is its
     significance in the history of the NT text?
4   Describe the developments in NT textual criticism up to the middle
     and later stages of the nineteenth century which made it inevitable
     that the position of the TR would be challenged.
5   Give the names of some of the significant scholars of this period and
     briefly describe their individual contributions.

Chapter 3

WESTCOTT AND HORT

The landmark names of modern textual criticism are B.F. Westcott (1825-1901) and F.J.A. Hort (1828-1892), both professors at the University of Cambridge and Westcott also the Anglican Bishop of Durham from 1890. Their efforts were devoted to formulating a text-critical methodology, making use of the discoveries of their predecessors. In 1881 they published their work in two volumes, one containing the NT text which was a complete departure from the TR, and the other an introduction in which they explained the principles on which their text was based. This introduction was essentially written by Hort but with his colleague's agreement.

It is true that much of Westcott and Hort's work was anticipated by others (as illustrated in the previous chapter and also emphasised with a rather Germanic pedantry by K. and B. Aland in their book *The Text of the New Testament*). But there is no denying that Westcott and Hort gave clear expression to text-critical principles in a way not done before and their work has made a lasting impact. For this reason this whole chapter is given to a statement of their principles, and the following paragraphs attempt to provide a simplified summary of some of these.

Part II sets out "The Methods of Textual Criticism" (pages 19-72). First, there is discussion of the Internal Evidence of Readings, that is, individual readings considered in isolation. There are two main criteria. (a) Intrinsic Probability: the instinctive choice between readings on the basis of what seems the best sense, what a scholar judges the author most likely to have written. They acknowledge that this is a subjective tool with unreliable results. (b) Transcriptional Probability: the reading which best explains the existence of other readings, asking what change(s) a scribe is likely to have made (but often there are conflicting criteria which can be applied). This criterion assumes a presumption against readings likely to have commended themselves to scribes.

These two criteria are often in conflict, because a reading that is to us intrinsically probable (leading to the conclusion that this is what the original author wrote) may have been equally attractive to a scribe (leading to the conclusion that this is likely to be a scribal change).

This type of evidence is inadequate to solve textual problems, and so we come to the Internal Evidence of Documents. The credibility of the documents in which the readings are found must be determined. To determine credibility: (a) relative age is a preliminary consideration; (b) internal evidence of readings will suggest relative credibility or the opposite. For example, if the study of individual variants shows that a particular MS consistently contains the preferred variant over many passages, this indicates a MS of good quality and reliability. This is summarised in the principle that "knowledge of documents should precede final judgement upon readings" (page 31).

Unfortunately, documents are not homogeneous, because of (a) having an excellence of one kind but corruptness of another, (b) different books within a MS being derived from different exemplars, (c) a mixture of exemplars for the text of even a single NT book. The first of these points means that a MS may be well copied by a careful scribe but from a poor exemplar, or (conversely) be based on a good quality exemplar but show careless scribal work and thus contain many mistakes.

And so, again, this type of evidence is inconclusive, and we are led to the matter of <u>Genealogical Evidence</u>. Genealogical affinities between documents need to be discovered. The mere number of MSS is not in itself significant. Another major text-critical principle is derived from these considerations: "All trustworthy restoration of corrupted texts is founded on the study of their history" (page 40).

In Part III ("Application of Principles of Criticism to the Text of the New Testament") Westcott and Hort summarise the <u>Results of Genealogical Evidence</u> by arguing that all the main forms of text were in existence prior to the 5th century. The text of Chrysostom and other Syrian Fathers of the 4th century is substantially identical with the common late text. The text of other major groups of texts is no later and in some cases comes from the second or third century. That the Syrian text is later than the Western, Alexandrian and Neutral text is shown by (a) analysis of conflate readings, (b) ante-Nicene patristic readings, and (c) internal evidence of Syrian readings. A conflate reading occurs when a scribe knows of two variants and instead of choosing one or the other simply combines the two into a single combined (or conflate) reading; a variant that represents a conflate reading is therefore always later than other variants.

Later in this same part a description is given of the <u>Characteristics of the Chief Ancient Texts</u> (pages 119-135):

<u>Western</u>. This is characterised by paraphrase involving even whole sentences and a readiness to adopt extraneous matter; also (though in

these points not unique) by more minor forms of paraphrase and assimilation (harmonistic corruption).

Neutral. The purest available form of the NT text, to be distinguished from a broader Alexandrian text.

Alexandrian. There is a distinct class of Alexandrian readings, derived from other non-Western pre-Syrian (ie neutral) readings and not vice versa. It is characterised by minor (but not bold) forms of paraphrase and by skillful assimilation; it lacks extraneous interpolations.

Syrian. An edition formed from its three chief predecessors. Its probable origin was the inconvenient conflict of the earlier texts, the choice of readings for the Syrian text based on a rough kind of intrinsic probability. Its chief qualities are lucidity and completeness, with little omitted from earlier texts but much added, with a resulting smoothness and loss of force.

The major uncial MSS known to Westcott and Hort are classified as follows:

Sinaiticus (ℵ): Pre-Syrian, with large Western and Alexandrian elements.

Alexandrinus (A): A mixed text. In the Gospels predominantly Syrian; in the other books readings of all types, with Alexandrian readings outnumbering Western readings in Acts and the epistles.

Vaticanus (B): Here is WH's own description. "We have not been able to recognise as Alexandrian any readings of B in any book of the New Testament which it contains; so that, with the exceptions already noticed, to the best of our belief neither of the early streams of innovation has touched it to any appreciable extent. This peculiar character is exhibited to the eye in the documentary evidence of those variations in which both a Western and an Alexandrian corruption is present, and one of these corruptions is adopted in the Syrian text, B then being conspicuous in the usually slender array supporting the reading from which both have diverged. It must not of course be assumed to follow that B has remained unaffected by sporadic corruption independent of the three great lines, Western, Alexandrian, and Syrian. In the Gospel of Matthew for instance it has occasionally admitted widely spread readings of very doubtful genuineness. But the influence of these three lines upon almost all extant documents has been so enormous that the highest interest must already be seen to belong to a document of which thus far we know only that its text is not only pre-Syrian but substantially free from Western and

Alexandrian adulteration" (pages 150-151). This quotation gives the reader a taste of Westcott and Hort's English style, which tends to be difficult for many modern readers of English. But in summary, they are saying that though Vaticanus has its faults, it lacks the secondary readings which are seen not only in the late Syrian text form but also in the earlier text forms (ie the Western and Alexandrian). The fact that the vast majority of MSS *do* reveal such secondary readings (to a greater or lesser extent) makes Vaticanus stand out as having a special quality.

Ephraemi Rescriptus (C): The Syrian and all three forms of pre-Syrian text are combined in various proportions.

Bezae (D in the Gospels and Acts): A Western text of the 2nd century, with some 4th century readings.

Claromontanus (D in Paul): Similarly Western.

Regarding the Post-Nicene History of the text Westcott and Hort speak of two stages of the Syrian text which can be discerned (indicated by minor differences of reading): (a) the first Syrian revision, of uncertain date, between AD 250 and 350, and possibly made or promoted by Lucian of Antioch (late 3rd century); (b) a second form, dominant from the end of the 4th century. Relics of earlier texts continued to be included in otherwise Syrian MSS for some time, but increasingly these were removed and only the Syrian text was copied. Prior to the invention of printing the victory of the Syrian text was all but complete.

For the material of this chapter, see further Metzger & Ehrman, 174-183; Aland, 14-18; Comfort, 100; E.J. Epp in Epp & Fee, chapter 2.

Revision Questions

1   In what ways did Westcott and Hort represent a change of direction in NT textual studies?
2   Give an outline of the three major stages of Westcott and Hort's approach to identifying the original text of the NT. Explain each stage as fully as you can.
3   Describe the major forms of text identified by Westcott and Hort, and the relative value of each text-type.
4   For Westcott and Hort which Greek MS is the closest to the original NT text? On what grounds did they come to this conclusion?
5   What was Westcott and Hort's attitude to the *Textus Receptus*?

Chapter 4

THE TWENTIETH CENTURY AND BEYOND

Westcott and Hort's labours did not bring the quest for the original NT text to an end. Despite the description of their publication as the "New Testament in the *Original* Greek", this claim was by no means accepted at face value and it was recognised that much more work was needed. It is not possible to cover every scholar, or even every *significant* scholar, but some of the more important names and events of the twentieth century and the early twenty-first century must be mentioned.

Reactions to Westcott and Hort

Even before the end of the 19th century we find conservative opposition to Westcott and Hort (WH), centred in the writings of J.W. Burgon whose views have been revived more recently (as we will see later). Burgon's response was basically a theological objection, namely that God in his providence would not have allowed an inferior text to become the one used by the church for so many centuries. Burgon's basic principle is that the majority is always right. Other critics were more reasoned in their response to WH. F.H.A. Scrivener objected to the total rejection of the Syrian text and G. Salmon argued for a greater consideration of Western readings. But despite such reactions WH's work paved the way for new editions of the Greek NT which did not follow the TR.

Early twentieth century developments

In 1908 C.R. Gregory published a list of MSS using the system of notation still in use today: papyri were numbered $\mathfrak{P}^1$ and so on, uncials 01 and so on (with a zero prefixed to the Arabic numeral, as well as the existing alphabet system which applies as far as codex 045), minuscules 1 and so on (a simple Arabic numeral), and the lectionaries l^1 and so on. Gregory himself was responsible for the discovery as well as the cataloguing of many MSS. His catalogue includes over 4,000 items, compared to only 1,000 known before Tischendorf. This reveals the massive growth in resources available for textual criticism.

H. von Soden published an edition of the Greek text in 1913, but his main importance is his work on text groupings. His classification of text-types (into an H text [Egyptian; H = Ἡσύχιος], an I text [Jerusalem; I = Ἱεροσόλυμα] and a K text [Koine or Byzantine; K = Κοινή]) has not been widely accepted, but the vast amount of data which he assembled, especially on MSS belonging to the K text-type, continue to be valuable.

A.C. Clark (*The Primitive Text of the Gospels and Acts*, 1914) is one of several scholars who have given a much more significant place to the Western text than Westcott and Hort did. Clark believed (contrary to most textual critics before or after) that scribes tended to omit (rather than add) sections of text, and so the longer text of the Western tradition has a greater claim to originality than WH's Neutral text. His views have not been accepted by others, although some have taken a positive attitude to the Western text on other grounds.

B.H. Streeter (*The Four Gospels*, 1924) used quotations from the Fathers to produce a theory of "local texts": Alexandrian (deriving from Alexandria), Eastern (deriving from Antioch) and Western (deriving from Rome). The Byzantine text was a revision based on these earlier forms of text. Streeter emphasised the importance of noting the geographical spread of witnesses for a reading. An influential part of Streeter's theory was his identification of a "Caesarean" text, a branch of his Eastern text.

The papyri

Gregory's catalogue (1908) mentions only fourteen known papyri containing NT text. Since then major papyrus discoveries have been made. In the 1930s the Chester Beatty papyri were published, including $\mathfrak{P}^{45}$, $\mathfrak{P}^{46}$ and $\mathfrak{P}^{47}$. Soon afterwards C.H. Roberts published $\mathfrak{P}^{52}$, only a few verses of John's Gospel but dated no later than AD 125 and thus very early evidence of the existence of this Gospel. The other major collection is the Bodmer papyri ($\mathfrak{P}^{66}$, $\mathfrak{P}^{72}$, $\mathfrak{P}^{74}$ and $\mathfrak{P}^{75}$). All of these have made a significant difference to our understanding of the history of the NT text.

See further E.J. Epp, in Ehrman & Holmes, chapter 1.

The minuscules

The large number of minuscule MSS has already been noted, but adequate study of these in proper detail has proved a major challenge. The overwhelming quantity of minuscules has been a problem in itself, and this situation has not been helped by an awareness that these MSS are relatively late and for the most part represent the Byzantine text. It has been easy to feel that the time and effort required to study these MSS adequately are not worthwhile.

However, it has also long been recognised that not all minuscule MSS are identical. They represent varieties of the Byzantine text, and in some cases contain readings of other text-types. So it is not appropriate simply to put all minuscules into a single category (late and Byzantine) and then ignore them. Much work has been done through the application of the Claremont Profile Method, a method of identifying the characteristic readings of a MS in relation to other MSS and so enabling MSS to be appropriately grouped. K. and B. Aland and others at the Münster Institute in Germany have also worked on analysing the text of the minuscules. The introduction to UBS[5] (page 5*) mentions the Coherence-Based Genealogical Method as a new approach for evaluating the Greek witnesses, with a brief explanation on the same page; see further on page 29 of this book.

See further B. Aland and K. Wachtel, in Ehrman & Holmes, chapter 3.

<u>Editions of the twentieth and early twenty-first century</u>

In 1898 Eberhard Nestle published the first edition of his *Novum Testamentum Graece*, with many other editions to follow. This text was based on the editions of Tischendorf (who relied heavily on Sinaiticus) and Westcott and Hort (for whom Vaticanus was preeminent). Where these two differed, Nestle used a third text to decide the matter. B. Weiss published an edition (1894-1900), and it was this which was used by Nestle as his third source text from 1901 onwards. Since Weiss also had a high regard for Vaticanus, it is not surprising that there was a close resemblance between the Nestle and WH texts. Nestle's work was continued by his son Erwin Nestle from the 13th edition (1927), and from the 21st edition (1951) K. Aland has been associated with this publication. That is how this text has become known as the Nestle-Aland (NA) text. The 25th edition (a text with a relatively small number of 558 differences from WH's text) was published in 1963 (26th edition, 1979; 27th edition, 1993; 28th edition, 2012).

Some other editions of the twentieth century deserve mention. A. Souter (1st edition, 1910; 2nd edition with the same text, 1947) produced a text which used the TR as its base (a 1550 edition of the TR published by Stephanus) but was altered to reflect the Greek text underlying the English Revised Version of 1881 (RV). Though one might think that this would look like WH's text more or less, it followed the principle of not changing from the TR in places where the RV translation could equally be derived from either TR or WH, and so it actually was much more like the TR than any other widely used text (as well as retaining some of the typographical and orthographical peculiarities of Stephanus' text). The British and

Foreign Bible Society for many years printed the 1624 Elzevir text, with slight differences, but as part of its centenary celebrations in 1904 used the text of Nestle's 4th edition of that year. A revision of this with fewer than twenty changes to the text was issued in 1958 and was widely used. The United Bible Societies published their first edition in 1966, with the needs of Bible translators especially in mind (2nd edition, 1968; 3rd edition, 1975, 4th edition, 1993). Widely used editions in the Roman Catholic church include those produced by H.J. Vogels (1st edition, 1922), A. Merk (1st edition, 1933) and J.M. Bover (1st edition, 1943).

The editions now in common use are the United Bible Societies 5th edition (UBS[5]) (2014) and the Nestle-Aland 28th edition (NA[28]) (2012). More will be said about these in later chapters.

Other recent editions include the SBL Greek New Testament (2010), an edition produced by M.W. Holmes, based on the WH text and essentially a consensus of WH, Tregelles, the Greek text underlying the 1984 NIV, and the Majority Text. The apparatus does not record textual data from Greek MSS or other witnesses, but merely reports differences when one or more of the above texts differs from the text which is printed. Another is the Crossway Greek New Testament (2017), published by Tyndale House, Cambridge. Its distinctive characteristic is that its text is based on Tregelles' edition, but its apparatus is of limited value compared to UBS[5] and NA[28], as it records many fewer variants than NA[28] (in Mark 1 it has 16 apparatus units compared with NA[28]'s 73) and cites fewer witnesses than either of the other two editions. It is interesting that both these editions give prominence to the often neglected work of S.P. Tregelles.

The above mentioned editions can be described as "manual" editions, that is, smaller editions suitable for regular use by students and pastors. But as well as these, editions of parts of the NT on a much larger scale have been published, with varying degrees of acceptance. S.C.E. Legg published editions of Mark (1935) and Matthew (1940) in the *Novum Testamentum Graece secundum Textum Westcotto-Hortianum* edition. His work on Luke was not published, but was utilised by The International Greek New Testament Apparatus Project, which took more than forty years to publish their work on Luke (1984-87). The work of preparing a major critical edition (with textual data presented as fully as possible) is now being undertaken by the Münster textual research institute, under the title *Novum Testamentum Graecum - Editio Critica Maior* (Greek New Testament Major Critical Edition). Volume 4 of this project has appeared, covering the catholic epistles (James to Jude), with a 2nd (revised) edition of this volume published in 2012.

The digital revolution

Much material is now available digitally. For example, on the Crosswire Bible Society's website (crosswire.org), it is possible to access many older publications as well as up to date editions. Material which may otherwise be difficult to access includes the Textus Receptus (various editions), Tischendorf's 8th edition, Tregelles' text, WH (with the variants of UBS[4] and NA[27]), and the Byzantine/Majority text. Many ancient versions are available on the same site. The same website has links to recent editions such as NA[28] (though not the apparatus) and the SBL text. Other useful websites are logos.com (Logos Bible Software), biblia.com, and ntgateway.com (New Testament Gateway).

Comments about web-based resources are out of date almost as soon as they are made, with constant changes taking place. In addition to what has already been mentioned, images of MSS can be found, and many articles related to textual criticism. Students will no doubt do their own searches, and, as with all web-based material, need to learn to be discriminating and to check that the sources of information and comments are reliable.

See further Metzger & Ehrman, 183-194; Aland, 19-26; Comfort, 101-102; M. Silva, in Ehrman & Holmes, chapter 18.

Revision Questions

1   Describe some of the reactions (scholarly and otherwise) to Westcott and Hort's work.
2   What were some of the major achievements of textual critics in the twentieth century?
3   List some of the important editions of the Greek NT published from 1898 onwards, with the major characteristics of each.

Chapter 5

ATTEMPTS TO UNDERSTAND
THE DEVELOPMENT OF THE TEXT

Westcott and Hort offered a clear description of their understanding of the history of the New Testament text, starting from a demonstration that the Byzantine (in their terminology "Syrian") text was a creation of the 4th century, derived from earlier forms of the text. These earlier forms are described as Alexandrian and Western, and both of these also reveal "corruptions" from an earlier standard. They identified Vaticanus (B) as a text relatively free of corruptions, and so labelled this as the "Neutral" text. Contrary to some popular and simplistic presentations, they did *not* regard Vaticanus as perfectly pure. Nor did they equate the Neutral text of B with the Alexandrian text, but regarded the latter as a later and corrupted version. Inevitably, WH's views were based on the great uncials of the 4th century and later, taking into account evidence from some of the versions also; the papyri were virtually unknown in their time.

We have already observed some of the initial reactions to WH's views. The discoveries of the past century and further analysis of the evidence have led to at least the following disagreements with WH: (a) Byzantine readings have been discovered in earlier witnesses (eg $\mathfrak{P}^{46}$, 3rd century), requiring some revision regarding the Byzantine text. However, it is not surprising if distinctive Byzantine readings are occasionally found in earlier sources. This does not invalidate the creation of the Byzantine text-type as such in the 4th century. (b) Scholars have generally rejected WH's distinction between the Alexandrian text and the Neutral text, and WH's exalted view of the value of Vaticanus. Instead they see Vaticanus as an early witness of the Alexandrian text-type, and without the same privileged status as WH gave it. (c) There is now not such a negative view of the Western text as we find in WH. Though some have given the Western text the same position which WH gave to the Neutral text, most have not gone to that extreme. Nevertheless scholars are much more open to consider the possibility that the Western text contains readings worthy of serious consideration. (d) The papyri have provided new evidence for the earlier period which was not available to WH, and these have enabled new views of the early history to be suggested.

The papyri have allowed the previously identified text-types to be traced back to an earlier period. Scholars are more likely to speak about textual complexions or trajectories (than about "types", which suggests something formally created and relatively fixed). So, for example, we have the following description offered by E.J. Epp (in Ehrman & Holmes, chapter 1; also in Epp & Fee, chapters 2 and 14):

1   B-text group: $\mathfrak{P}^{75}$ $\mathfrak{P}^{66}$ B $\aleph$ (except in John) L 33, plus (for Paul) $\mathfrak{P}^{46}$ 1739.
2   D-text group: $\mathfrak{P}^{48}$ $\mathfrak{P}^{38}$ $\mathfrak{P}^{69}$ (possibly $\mathfrak{P}^{29}$) 0171, with D 1739 (in Acts) 614 383.
3   C-text group (Gospels) (midway between the B and D groups): $\mathfrak{P}^{45}$ W family 13.
4   A-text group (the later Majority or Byzantine group): A (Gospels only), later papyri ($\mathfrak{P}^{84}$, 6th century; $\mathfrak{P}^{68}$ and perhaps $\mathfrak{P}^{74}$, 7th; $\mathfrak{P}^{42}$, 7th/8th).

These groups seem to correspond roughly to the groups previously labelled (respectively) as Alexandrian, Western, Caesarean and Byzantine, so that in a sense the papyri have not radically changed the picture but only taken us a step earlier in the historical process. But others will claim more significant differences between a WH-type evaluation and a contemporary understanding, with the following comments (among others): (a) Text-types should not be rigidly defined, but greater attention needs to be given to variations within a group, that is, to the particular readings of individual witnesses; hence the preference for terminology such as "textual trajectories" rather than "text-types". (b) In particular it is impossible to think of the Western text as a homogeneous text, but a text with many unusual readings, and with much variety among Western witnesses. It is also impossible to regard it as strictly western in a geographical sense, as "Western" characteristics occur in witnesses geographically located in the east. (c) Doubts must exist about a clearly defined C-text (Caesarean). (This type was not, of course, part of WH's understanding, but originated with B.H. Streeter.)

More detailed study of some of the Fathers has allowed further refinements to be suggested. G.D. Fee's study of the text of John in Origen and Cyril of Alexandria (in Epp & Fee, chapter 15) has led him to identify four levels of Alexandrian witnesses (surprisingly he uses the word "Neutral"), with an increasing number of Byzantine readings in the course of time, as seen especially in the witnesses of levels three and four:

1    $\mathfrak{P}^{75}$ B Origen.
2    $\mathfrak{P}^{66}$ C.
3   L 33 Cyril.
4   Ψ 579 892 1241.

This table shows that MSS continued to be made from Alexandrian exemplars, but with an increasing amount of Byzantine mixture, which is not surprising considering the growing dominance of the Byzantine text.

What general picture emerges? G.D. Fee (in Epp & Fee, chapter 1) speaks of the first 400 years as a period of confusion, when the vast majority of textual changes were made. This applies especially to the 2nd century, "when each NT book was being transmitted independently of the others and when there was wide geographical distribution of these documents with little or no 'controls'" (page 9). Though it may be possible to talk about text groups (as described above), there were no "editions" as such. Text groups from this period must therefore be regarded as loose groupings. On the other hand the Byzantine text is a much more clearly defined text-type. This text (as distinct from earlier attested readings which were later incorporated in the Byzantine text) emerges during the 4th century, though with much uncertainty about its actual origin.

The previous paragraph was described as a "general picture". None of this specifically answers the question regarding the *original* text. In fact it raises the question whether we know enough to be able to recover the original text. If we only know that the 2nd century in particular was a "period of confusion", we are left with the possibly discouraging question how we identify *original* readings in the midst of this confusion.

However, other scholars are less pessimistic. P. Comfort has made a useful contribution to this debate. In *Encountering the Manuscripts*, 255-279, he has made a detailed study of the papyri (that is, the earliest textual evidence on the whole) and agrees with others that it is not possible to speak of early text-types. Each papyrus document bears its own witness to the early history of the text and needs to be studied separately in order to evaluate its textual reliability. He helpfully lists the papyri which can be dated before AD 300 and classifies them as "reliable", "fairly reliable" and "unreliable" (pages 268-270). He also disagrees with scholars (for example, Fee and Ehrman) who describe the early period as one of uncontrolled transmission of the text. It is not as simple as that, for many papyrus MSS reveal great care in copying (in the Alexandrian tradition of reproducing ancient texts, secular as well as religious) and though it is not possible to claim that any of them represents the original text exactly, there is good reason to be confident that we have enough reliable early evidence to take us very close to the original wording.

Aspects of WH's theory which have generally been abandoned (or at least significantly modified) by modern scholars have been noted above.

Nevertheless, it is interesting to note that WH's text was taken as the basis for the text of UBS[4] and NA[27] (*Textual Commentary*, 10*). The recently published NA[28] (2012) and UBS[5] (2014) have begun to move away from this text, but only in a small number of cases in the general epistles (in fact there are only 34 changes to the text of UBS[5] compared with UBS[4], and many of these are quite minor). This does not mean that the text now in common use is the same as WH, but it does suggest that to a major extent WH's results have stood the test of time. For example, Vaticanus is still regarded very highly by most textual critics, and the papyri (discovered since the time of WH) which are earlier than Vaticanus have tended to confirm the overall reliability of Vaticanus. This explains why WH's 1881 text and UBS[4]'s 1993 text (and indeed UBS[5]'s 2014 text) have so much in common. All this suggests that there has been not so much an *abandonment* of WH as some *modifications*, significant as these may be.

In addition to material already noted, some further interesting observations (not always in agreement with the picture presented above) are contained in Aland, 48-71.

Revision Questions

1   Give a brief outline of Westcott and Hort's understanding of the history of the NT text, as evidenced in the witnesses available to them.

2   Identify the factors which have caused a reassessment of Westcott and Hort's picture.

3   What effect have the papyri had on our understanding of the transmission of the text of the NT?

4   Describe G.D. Fee's picture of the development of the Alexandrian text-type.

5   What marks the Byzantine text-type as fundamentally different from the earlier types of text that have been identified?

6   What would you say is the current status of the Westcott and Hort text?

Chapter 6

ATTEMPTS TO RECOVER THE TEXT

In this chapter we will seek to summarise the story up to the present time and to discuss the views of contemporary scholars about the best method or methods to obtain the original text of the NT or at least the earliest form which we can reach.

Eclecticism

The major debate in contemporary textual criticism relates to the subject of eclecticism. This method has arisen from the perceived failure of WH's method to reach back to the original text. Even if we accept that WH's approach has given us access to text forms of the 2nd century, that is still not the *original* text. Is there another method offering hope of better results? Eclecticism comes in two main forms, but both move away from too great a dependence on tracing the genealogical relationships of the MSS. We will remind ourselves of WH's approach and then look at the two forms of eclecticism.

The WH approach can be described as a historical-genealogical approach, which places great weight on external criteria, namely the value of the MSS and of MS groupings. This involves an attempt to reconstruct the history of the text and to make textual decisions on the basis of what are considered the earliest and most reliable witnesses (though our summary of WH in chapter 3 has shown that they also used internal criteria much more than is sometimes recognised).

The first type of eclecticism is known as thoroughgoing eclecticism, which fully relies on internal criteria. It is not interested in the historical development of text-types or genealogical relationships or the quality of a MS, but deals only with the available readings themselves. Its results are based on scholars' assessment of these, in terms of what an author is most likely to have written and the sorts of changes scribes are most likely to have made. Eclecticism is derived from the Greek verb meaning "choose", and in the context of *thoroughgoing* eclecticism it refers to the method of deciding a reading by choosing from any of the available readings. This theory means that even a single late minuscule, from none of the earlier groupings, might preserve the original reading in opposition to all the other testimony. It is argued that, since virtually all variants were created by AD 200, it does not matter whether the available source of a variant is a

4th or 7th or 10th century witness, because the reading will have been in existence before AD 200 anyway. This consideration, it is claimed, makes external evidence virtually irrelevant. But most scholars are unwilling to accept this assessment of the external evidence. The argument that most variants were in existence by AD 200 cannot lead to the conclusion that all extant MSS are therefore equally corrupt or that none is more reliable than any other. On thoroughgoing eclecticism, see further J.K. Elliott, in Ehrman & Holmes, chapter 20, and in Black, chapter 3.

Another form of eclecticism is known as <u>reasoned eclecticism</u>. This third approach is really a mixture of the other two approaches just described. It is willing to consider external criteria as well as internal criteria. Here eclecticism has a different application, for this method is "eclectic" in the sense that it chooses among all the available criteria when making a textual decision. Sometimes preference will be given to internal criteria and sometimes to external criteria.

This more moderate form of eclecticism is what most textual critics actually use today. The basic rule of reasoned eclecticism has been expressed in these terms: "The variant most likely to be original is the one that best accounts for the origin of all the competing variants, in terms of both external and internal evidence" (M.W. Holmes, in Ehrman & Holmes, 344-345). Here Holmes mentions both external and internal criteria. Regarding external criteria, it is felt that even if we cannot be sure of the *original* text, it is still proper to use external evidence to try to identify the *earliest available* form or forms of the text. Then, if the application of external criteria leaves us with two or more alternatives, internal criteria must be used to make a choice.

But there are difficulties regarding the internal criteria. Various studies have been done on some of these criteria, and M.W. Holmes (in the same article) comments that "the cumulative effect of many of these studies has been to weaken or require extensive modification of several of the traditional criteria" (page 343), such as the shorter reading principle, an author's style, Atticistic tendencies, and the view that deliberate changes were made only by heretics. "The primary effect of recent discussions of the various criteria, including the efforts to improve or refine them, has been to increase our skepticism. We are less sure than ever that their use, no matter how sophisticated, will produce any certainty with regard to the results obtained" (page 343). On reasoned eclecticism, see further M.W. Holmes, in Ehrman & Holmes, chapter 21, and in Black, chapter 2.

The word "subjectivity" sums up the problems of eclecticism. *Thorough-going* eclecticism is totally dependent on a scholar's assessment of what the original author wrote. When one realises the large amount of disagreement among writers of NT commentaries, it is difficult to believe that a textual critic has infallible knowledge of what the author would certainly have written. Such an approach assumes that we have a much more intimate acquaintance with an ancient author's mind than we actually do. *Reasoned* eclecticism suffers from several related problems. (a) To give consideration to both internal and external criteria appears to be a well-balanced approach, but there is no clear-cut guidance which of the two types of criteria should be given greater importance. (b) The internal criteria are still far from satisfactorily defined (see Holmes' comments reported above). (c) These criteria are sometimes in conflict with each other. All these factors require subjective assessments on the part of textual critics. It is all very well saying that textual criticism is an art as well as a science, but the more it is art, the more subjectivity enters the picture. In such circumstances it seems difficult to claim that eclectic methods have produced greater certainty than WH reached regarding the original text of the NT. We can criticise WH if we wish, but modern methods of textual criticism do not seem to rest on any stronger foundation.

The Alands' local-genealogical method

Kurt Aland and Barbara Aland have been significant textual critics during the last half of the twentieth century. Despite the enormous contribution they have made, some of their views (which we note briefly) are considered eccentric by other scholars. Most scholars seem to regard the Alands as practitioners of reasoned eclecticism, though they themselves do not want to be labelled thus. They prefer to call their method the "local-genealogical method" (page 34). "Local" in this context refers to particular variants (not geographical localities), and it is at this local level of individual passages (rather than the broader level of complete MSS) that one can discover genealogical relationships. They attempt to trace genealogical relationships in individual passages (how one reading gave rise to another, and the relationships of readings within the same passage), but they do not consider it possible to trace broader genealogical relationships among the MSS.

Consistent with this, they also insist on seeing the papyri in isolation from the later traditions, thus ruling out the possibility of tracing relationships between the papyri and later forms of the text.

They offer a fivefold classification of MSS. This appears in three different places in their book, in slightly different wording in each place, first on page 106 and then on page 159. What follows provides abbreviated quotations from pages 335-336:

Category I	"Manuscripts of a very special quality, ... with a very high proportion of the early text ... , presumably the original text."
Category II	"Manuscripts of a special quality, ... with a considerable proportion of the early text."
Category III	"Manuscripts with a small but not negligible proportion of early readings, with a considerable encroachment of polished readings (a relatively strong Byzantine influence), and significant readings from other sources as yet unidentified."
Category IV	Manuscripts of the D-text (Western text).
Category V	Manuscripts that are purely or predominantly Byzantine.

The basis for this classification is not consistent. The last two are "text-types" as traditionally understood. The other three are on the basis of MS quality, namely the proportion of early readings in a MS. This assumes that we know what an "early reading" is, which is surely the very thing textual critics are trying to discover. If the Alands already know what the early text is, it makes most of textual criticism irrelevant. It is hard to identify reasons for these definitions. One receives the impression that they consider their own opinion based on their familiarity with the MSS to be sufficient authority and justification for the conclusions they reach. However much one wishes to honour the expertise of such scholars, their own authority can hardly be accepted as an adequate basis for a textual theory.

It is also a problem when MSS are given a category I rating because of date, such as 0162 (3rd/4th century) and all the papyri of the first three centuries. To quote the Alands: "The papyri and uncials up to the third/fourth century belong here [ie in Category I] almost automatically because they represent the text of the early period" (page 159). This implies that an early date is sufficient to guarantee a high proportion of early text ("presumably the original text", as the Alands consider category I MSS to be), something which other textual critics hesitate to accept, especially because it is widely accepted that it was in the early centuries that the greater amount of textual variation arose. Considerations like these suggest that caution should be exercised when making use of these categories.

Nevertheless the Alands' categories remain of considerable practical usefulness. The first three categories serve to identify the relative amount of mixture in the non-Byzantine MSS, with category I MSS being the least mixed and category III MSS containing the greatest quantity of Byzantine readings. We can increase the practical value of the first three categories by removing controversial reference to the original text and suggesting the following redefinition of the categories:

Category I   MSS with an early type of text, with little or no Byzantine influence.

Category II   MSS also with an early type of text, but with a greater amount of Byzantine influence.

Category III   MSS with a proportion of early readings, but with much more Byzantine influence.

These definitions still do not indicate *which* early type of text. Metzger's classification (see appendix 1 and appendix 2 of this book) shows which ones have an Alexandrian basis, which ones have a Western basis, and which ones can be roughly described as "Caesarean" (ie with a mix of Alexandrian and Western).

It may be convenient to add here a comment about the recently developed Coherence-Based Genealogical Method (CBGM). Though the phrase "local genealogical" is not used in the CBGM literature (as far as I have been able to see), CBGM seems to take its starting point from the same principle. That is, you look first not at MSS as a whole but at individual variants and try to work out the line of development; for example, if in a given passage there are four variations, decide in which order they arose by explaining how one might have been derived from another, and thus determine which variant is the likely earliest reading or potential ancestor of the others. By doing this for a sufficient number of individual passages, you will then be able to see which MSS are likely to be the source or potential ancestor of other MSS. The whole process is similar to the Alands' local-genealogical approach, except that this last stage seeks to trace genealogical relationships among the MSS, thus moving beyond the Alands' insistence that genealogical relationships could only be identified for individual passages.

The preceding paragraph is a highly simplified summary of the CBGM. Analysis by this method is quite complex and requires highly sophisticated data analysis by computer. For further information, see the article by K. Wachtel, "The Coherence Method and History", in volume 20 of *TC: A Journal of Biblical Textual Criticism* (2015), and other articles in the same volume; also UBS[5], 5*, and NA[28], 52*.

The standard text in current use

Despite the differences in method between the Alands and other textual critics, it is interesting to observe that there is widespread agreement about the results. In fact the UBS[4] and NA[27] texts are identical, the same text as UBS[3] and NA[26] before them, and there are only a few differences in the more recent UBS[5] and NA[28]. Textual critics with different points of view (other than the extreme forms of thoroughgoing eclecticism) were involved in the production of these volumes, and yet working from different theoretical positions have been able to agree on the final product. Furthermore, this basic text has been commonly accepted since the 1970s (UBS[3] was published in 1975, and NA[26] in 1979). The reality is that in spite of differences in theoretical approach, the work of the Alands is a reasoned eclectic approach, utilising both internal and external criteria to reach textual decisions. And because their evaluation of the quality of the major MSS is not much different from the evaluation made by others, including WH, it is not surprising that the results are similar.

What is the significance of this widely accepted text? The editors of UBS[4] and NA[27] stress that they do not intend these editions to be regarded as the finally established text of the original NT. Thus, in the preface to UBS[4] (page vi) we read: "The text of the edition has remained unchanged. This should not be misunderstood to mean that the editors now consider the text as established." And similarly in NA[27] (page 45*): "It should naturally be understood that this text is a working text (in the sense of the century-long Nestle tradition): it is not to be considered as definitive, but as a stimulus to further efforts toward defining and verifying the text of the New Testament." These statements have been proved true with the publication of UBS[5] and NA[28], for these new editions demonstrate that textual critics are willing to make changes in the light of new evidence or new evaluations, including the use of the new Coherence-Based Genealogical Method (see page 29 above). But even so the text has not much changed.

Alongside the statements in the introductions of UBS[4] and NA[27], insisting that the text should not be considered finally established, we need to note several factors which produce a different and even contradictory impression. Thus, the Alands refer to category I MSS as those with a high proportion of original readings, implying that they know what the original readings were and implying also that we have virtually recovered the original text. We note also that in UBS[4] only 9 passages in the whole NT are given a {D} rating and only 7 in UBS[5], in contrast to 145 in UBS[3]. Thus, in Matthew, out of UBS[3]'s 13 {D} ratings, only one remains {D} in UBS[4] and UBS[5], 9 are upgraded to {C}, and 3 are simply printed without variant recorded (which implies an {A} rating). One also notices a much higher proportion of {A} ratings in the later editions: in the same Gospel UBS[3] has only 8 such passages whereas UBS[4] and UBS[5] have 31 (21 of which have been upgraded from {B} in UBS[3]). At the very least these figures suggest that the UBS editors have become much more confident of the accuracy and originality of their text. One can only guess at the reasons for this growth in confidence, considering that there were no major MS discoveries or other advances in text-critical method in that period. No explanation of this increased confidence is given either in the introduction to UBS[4] or UBS[5] or in the accompanying *Textual Commentary* (2nd edition). It is hard to avoid the conclusion that there has been a move towards a new "textus receptus" in spite of denials of this by prominent textual critics.

This form of the text has been the one most readily accessible to a whole generation of NT scholars, and so it is natural to feel that this is *the* text of the NT, regardless of what is stated in the introductory comments in UBS[4] and NA[27]. Although NT scholars refer to variant readings when they discuss passages, one often finds that they choose the reading in the UBS/NA text, and that they justify this on the basis of reasons provided in the *Textual Commentary*. But since the *Textual Commentary* was written to justify the choice of the reading printed in the text, there is clearly a circular argument in operation here. One suspects that in the NT scholarly community there has been a *de facto* acceptance of the UBS[4]/NA[27] text as original. (For a description of the evolution of this text, see Aland, 30-36.)

The preceding comments require only slight modification in the light of the recently published NA[28] (2012) and UBS[5] (2014). The text of this edition is the same as UBS[4] and NA[27], except in the catholic epistles from James through to Jude, where the text has been modified according to the text published in the *Editio Critica Maior*. The latest UBS and NA show a willingness to incorporate changes, even if not a large number. No doubt it will be some time before the *ECM* is completed for all books of the NT, and we may have to wait till then in order to see how different the texts of the future will be compared with the standard texts of today. The text and textual apparatus of UBS[5] is discussed further in chapter 11, and a full list of the new readings is given in appendix 3.

Meanwhile we note that E.J. Epp has described the twentieth century as an interlude in NT textual criticism (in Epp & Fee, chapters 5 and 6). Though others (particularly the Alands) have strenuously objected to this claim, it is hard to deny in the light of the fact that the text now in common use (regarded by some as virtually the original text) is so closely related to the text claimed in 1881 as being the "original Greek". It cannot be denied that much labour has been devoted to different aspects of textual studies, and changes are slowly being introduced, but Epp is surely justified in asking for evidence of substantial advance.

The fact that we had identical texts for almost 40 years in the two most widely used editions and only a small number of changes in the most recent editions seems to suggest that reasoned eclecticism has reached the limits of its usefulness. This could be seen as a positive outcome, if the result is something very close to the original NT text. But this is not the conclusion drawn by textual critics, who see the task as very much unfinished. What then is the way forward? Major new discoveries of MSS could change the picture, but otherwise a different approach to textual criticism might be desirable. P. Comfort claims that current textual criticism places too much weight on internal evidence over external evidence, and that a greater focus on the external would be beneficial (see Comfort, 302-306). The following statement is worth quoting (page 306):

> Textual critics who have worked with many actual manu-scripts – both of the proto-Alexandrian type and the so-called Western type – in the task of compiling transcriptions and/or doing textual analysis and who have seen firsthand the kind of errors, expansions, harmonizations, and interpolations that are far more present in Western manuscripts, are convinced that manuscripts like $\mathfrak{P}^{75}$ and B represent the best of textual purity.

Remove the reference to $\mathfrak{P}^{75}$ and this sounds very much like WH! Of course we cannot simply return to WH, in view of the massive amount of evidence discovered since their time. But not unlike WH, Comfort, in the following pages of his discussion (pages 306-320), offers suggestions on how to identify the most accurate or best MSS and on refining the documentary method of textual criticism. The Coherence-Based Genealogical Method (see above, page 29), used in the preparation of the *ECM* volume, and therefore also of UBS[5] and NA[28], also recognises that MS quality is a significant factor, and perhaps holds out hope that future results will be more strongly based on external evidence. Such results could be claimed to be more objective than the current results based on reasoned eclecticism with all its subjectivity.

Whatever the future may hold, we may even now wish to rejoice that, despite the great amount of effort invested by textual critics towards the goal of recovering the NT text, there has been such a stable text from the time of WH till now, and that suggested changes are relatively few in number and minor in significance. Some might conclude that there is not much more that textual criticism can achieve apart from some tidying up around the edges, and might see this as very good news indeed.

The Majority Text theory

Before we leave the story of the twentieth century, it is important to note the debate about the so-called Majority Text. This brings us back to the significance and status of the Textus Receptus. We have observed how as a result of Erasmus' edition this form of the text became the accepted standard for more than three centuries, so that when its status was challenged (especially by Westcott and Hort, building on the work of others before them), there was a furious reaction in certain conservative circles. In the first place the opposition to WH was led by J.W. Burgon.

Support for the Majority Text was revived in the 20th century, especially through the writings of Z.C. Hodges in the 1970s and later. D.B. Wallace (in Ehrman & Holmes, chapter 19, and many other articles) gives a helpful survey of the issues. The basic position is that the true text of the NT is to be found in the majority of MSS, which means the Byzantine text. This position is based on the theological argument that the God who inspired his word must have preserved it during the centuries, and that the form of the NT used by most Christians throughout history must be the original; the theological assumptions here are verbal inspiration and providential preservation. If a particular form of words (and only these words) is inspired, then it is reasonable to expect that the majority of MSS (ie some form of the Byzantine text) preserve these words. Thus, it is claimed, the conclusions of WH and other like-minded textual critics are false when they claim greater importance for other (non-Byzantine) MSS.

It is not difficult to point out the weaknesses in this position. First of all, it is impossible to conduct historical enquiry if one's position is decided in advance by theological considerations. Historical realities must be allowed their proper place in textual criticism. Secondly, it is strange that there are no Byzantine witnesses from the early centuries, if God has preserved the true text in the Byzantine text-form. The standard argument, that all such early Byzantine MSS have worn out through overuse, is a counsel of despair. Finally, supporters of the Majority Text position must explain why the Majority Text is not uniform. The Textus Receptus itself is not identical with the Majority Text, but is a late and peculiar form of it (because of Erasmus' editorial methods). And even in the earlier Byzantine MSS there are many textual variants. The form of the Byzantine text which has become the Majority Text became the "majority" only from the 9th century. We can in fact identify at least three major stages of the history of the Byzantine text, involving many Byzantine variants: (a) the earlier Byzantine MSS (from the 5th century), (b) the majority text MSS, which developed as the Byzantine text became more and more standardised (dating from the 9th century), and (c) the Textus Receptus (based on the few MSS used by Erasmus). The Majority Text supporters have no theoretical basis on which to judge among such variants within the Byzantine tradition.

As well as D.B. Wallace (mentioned above), see Comfort, 98; M.W. Holmes, in *Themelios*, Vol 8 No 2 (1983), 13-19; G.D. Fee, in Epp & Fee, chapter 10; for a sympathetic presentation of the Majority Text position, see M.A. Robinson, in Black, chapter 4, and in the appendix of his 2005 edition of the Byzantine text, edited with W.G. Pierpont (details of this can be found on page 163).

Revision Questions

1   What are the two senses in which the word eclecticism is used in textual criticism?
2   Is there a satisfactory form of eclecticism which could achieve the basic aims of NT textual criticism or is a different method needed?
3   Describe the attitude of the Alands to the genealogical approach to textual criticism.
4   What are the strengths and weaknesses of the Alands' classification of manuscripts?
5   Has NT textual criticism produced a new *textus receptus*?
6   Outline the weaknesses in the view that the Majority Text represents the original form of the NT.

PART II

THE PRACTICE OF TEXTUAL CRITICISM

Chapter 7

THE WORK OF THE SCRIBES

The major types of changes introduced by the scribes can be broadly described as unintentional (the result of mere human error) and intentional (where a scribe has tried to improve the text, correcting what he perceives to be an error in his exemplar). An attempt has been made to avoid examples which you can find in Metzger & Ehrman and Aland (there are some exceptions); page numbers for the relevant sections of these books are given for most of the headings in the following material.

Only occasionally has an explanatory comment been given for the different headings here. Most of the points will be reasonably obvious. For further explanation, you will need to refer to Metzger & Ehrman. Also be aware that not all these variants are recorded in UBS. For those which are not, you will usually find details in NA or the *Textual Commentary*.

More information on this subject can be found in Comfort, 322-329. On scribal habits, see also J.R. Royse, in Ehrman & Holmes, chapter 15.

Unintentional Changes

1   Errors of sight

    a   Misreading of similar letters (Metzger & Ehrman, 251-252; Aland, 283). Remember that the earliest MSS were written in uncial script, not in the small letters with which we are familiar in our modern printed editions.

        Eph 4:19   ἀπηλγηκότες (*having become callous*) and ἀπηλπικότες (*having lost hope*). Confusion caused by the similarity of ΓΗ (gamma + eta) and ΠΙ (pi + iota).

        2 Cor 5:3   ἐκδυσάμενοι (*having put off*) and ἐκλυσάμενοι (*having given up*). Confusion caused by the similarity of Δ (delta) and Λ (lambda).

b   Haplography: writing a word or letter once when it should have
     been written twice (caused by homoeoteleuton [the same ending
     in a nearby word or passage] or homoeoarcton [the same beginn-
     ing in a nearby word or passage]) (Metzger & Ehrman, 254;
     Aland, 283-285).

Mt 19:29   Omission of πατέρα ἤ in ἤ πατέρα ἤ μητέρα. The
            scribe's eye has skipped from one ἤ to the other.
Lk 6:48   Omission of διὰ τὸ καλῶς οἰκοδομῆσθαι αὐτήν. The
            preceding word is αὐτήν. The scribe's eye has
            skipped from one αὐτήν to the other.
Jn 10:39   Because of -ουν in the ending of the verb ἐζήτουν, a
            scribe might easily neglect to write οὖν. So ἐζήτουν
            οὖν has become simply ἐζήτουν.

c   Dittography: writing a word or letter twice when it should have
     been written only once (also caused by homoeoteleuton or
     homoeoarcton) (Metzger & Ehrman, 254; Aland, 283-285).

Lk 6:35   Instead of μηδὲν ἀπελπίζοντες (*expecting nothing in
            return*), the reading μηδένα ἀπελπίζοντες has arisen
            through careless addition of an extra alpha.
Jn 20:21   Words such as θεός, Ἰησοῦς and κύριος were
            sometimes written in abbreviated form. An original
            text αὐτοῖς could have become αὐτοῖς οις by
            dittography, with οις an abbreviation of ὁ Ἰησοῦς.
            Or an original αὐτοῖς οις could have been simplified
            to αὐτοῖς by haplography.

2   Errors of hearing

Errors considered under this heading might arise not only in the
actual dictation of a MS (in a scriptorium), but also through a scribe
repeating a word to himself, either audibly or in his mind.

a   Vowels (Metzger & Ehrman, 254-256; Aland, 286-287).

Certain vowels had identical (or near identical) sounds in
Hellenistic Greek: ι = η = υ = ει = οι = υι, and ε = αι, and ο = ω.
The possibility for confusion for scribes is obvious.

Mt 19:24   Confusion of κάμηλον (*camel*) and κάμιλον (*rope*).
Lk 16:12   Confusion of ὑμέτερον and ἡμέτερον (and many
            examples involving forms of ἡμεῖς and ὑμεῖς).

Jn 12:43 Confusion of ἤπερ and ὑπέρ.

Rom 14:19 Confusion of διώκωμεν and διώκομεν (and a similar famous example in Rom 5:1).

Eph 4:23-24 Confusion of ἀνανεοῦσθαι and ἐνδύσασθαι with ἀνανεοῦσθε and ἐνδύσασθε.

b Consonants (Metzger & Ehrman, 256-257).

Ac 27:39 Confusion of ἐξῶσαι (*drive ashore*) and ἐκσῶσαι (*bring safely*). It would have been very difficult for a scribe to hear any difference between these words.

1 Th 2:7 Confusion of νήπιοι (*infants*) and ἤπιοι (*gentle*). The preceding word is ἐγενήθημεν. A scribe would easily have thought there was only one nu when there should have been two (or alternatively, two when there should only have been one).

3 Errors of the mind

a Substitution of synonyms (Metzger & Ehrman, 257; Aland, 291).

Mk 14:24 ὑπέρ changed to περί.

Jn 16:13 ὁδηγήσει changed to διηγήσεται.

Col 2:12 βαπτισμῷ changed to βαπτίσματι.

b Sequence of words (Metzger & Ehrman, 257).

Mk 1:5 Reversal of prepositional phrases in ὑπ' αὐτοῦ ἐν τῷ Ἰορδάνῃ ποταμῷ.

c Transposition of letters (Metzger & Ehrman, 257).

Mk 14:65 Confusion of ἔλαβον and ἔβαλον.

d Assimilation to a parallel passage (Metzger & Ehrman, 257). Examples are given below under harmonising as *intentional* change. It does not seem clear how we can know whether such changes are unintentional (the result of subconscious familiarity with the parallel) or intentional.

4   Errors of judgment (Metzger & Ehrman, 258-259)

   a   Incorporation of marginal notes.

        Mk 7:16   The familiar words εἴ τις ἔχει ὦτα ἀκούειν ἀκουέτω
                     were perhaps written as a comment in the margin
                     and included in the text by a later scribe.
        Lk 17:9   The words οὐ δοκῶ (*I don't think so*) were probably
                     first written in the margin as a reader's amused res-
                     ponse to the question of this verse, and later added
                     to the text by a scribe.

   b   Wrong order of words.

        Lk 3:23-38   Instead of reading *down* each column of text, one
                     scribe apparently read *across* and thus created a
                     completely new (and incorrect) genealogy.

   c   Wrong division of words.

        Rom 7:14   Confusion between οἴδαμεν and οἶδα μέν.

Intentional Changes

Some of these may be the work of an individual scribe and some the result
of deliberate editing of the text at different stages of history.

1   Spelling, grammar and style (Metzger & Ehrman, 261-262; Aland,
       290).

        Mk 14:72   Changes made in order to avoid the clumsy
                     juxtaposition of the adverbs δὶς τρίς.
        Lk 5:17   Changing αὐτόν to αὐτούς or πάντας, failing to see that
                     αὐτόν is subject (not object) of ἰᾶσθαι.
        Lk 13:35   Unusual use of the subjunctive εἴπητε after ὅτε has led
                     to many attempted improvements.
        Lk 24:47   The nominative ἀρξάμενοι only works by being linked
                     with ὑμεῖς in verse 48 (UBS has punctuated thus). The
                     changes to other cases are attempts to improve the
                     syntax (eg ἀρξαμένων with an implied ὑμῶν, forming a
                     genitive absolute).
        Jn 8:39   Replacement of ἐστε with ἦτε, and addition of ἄν, are
                     attempts to improve the grammar in a contrary to fact
                     conditional statement.

Jn 13:26   Change from βάψω ... καὶ δώσω (more Semitic-like paratactic construction) to βάψας ... δώσω, subordinating one of the verbs, is a stylistic improvement.

Jn 16:13   Change from ὅσα ἀκούσει to ὅσα ἂν ἀκούσῃ as a more appropriate means of expressing an indefinite clause. Not in UBS; see the *Textual Commentary*.

2   Harmonising (Metzger & Ehrman, 262-263; Aland, 290).

The UBS apparatus identifies probable examples by including the likely parallel passage after the relevant variant. Most examples occur among the Synoptic Gospels, but there are also harmonisations with an OT passage, or between Ephesians and Colossians.

Mt 8:10	See Lk 7:9.	Lk 9:35	See Mk 9:7.
Mt 11:19	See Lk 7:35.	Lk 13:35	See Mt 23:39.
Mt 14:24	See Mk 6:46.	Col 1:14	See Eph 1:7.
Lk 4:18	See Is 61:1.	Col 3:6	See Eph 5:6.

3   Natural complements (Metzger & Ehrman, 263-264; Aland, 289-90).

Mt 22:30   ἄγγελοι has become ἄγγελοι (τοῦ) θεοῦ.

Jn 6:47   ὁ πιστεύων has become ὁ πιστεύων εἰς ἐμέ.

Jn 7:39   πνεῦμα has become πνεῦμα ἅγιον.

1 Cor 5:5   τοῦ κυρίου has become τοῦ κυρίου Ἰησοῦ or τοῦ κυρίου Ἰησοῦ Χριστοῦ or τοῦ κυρίου ἡμῶν Ἰησοῦ Χριστοῦ.

4   Historical and geographical difficulties (Metzger & Ehrman, 264).

Mk 5:1   There seems to have been widespread confusion about the correct name of the people of the area, as reflected in the variants.

Lk 24:13   Different views of the location of Emmaus have led to variants in the distance from Jerusalem.

Jn 1:28   Doubts about Bethany were expressed by Origen, and the alternative Bethabara has arisen.

5   Conflation (Metzger & Ehrman, 265; Aland, 293-294).

Mt 13:57   ἐν τῇ πατρίδι and ἐν τῇ πατρίδι αὐτοῦ and ἐν τῇ ἰδίᾳ πατρίδι have been combined into ἐν τῇ ἰδίᾳ πατρίδι αὐτοῦ.

Lk 24:53   εὐλογοῦντες and αἰνοῦντες have been combined.

Rom 6:12   ταῖς ἐπιθυμίαις αὐτοῦ and αὐτῇ have been combined
            into αὐτῇ ἐν ταῖς ἐπιθυμίαις αὐτοῦ.

Col 1:12   ἱκανώσαντι and καλέσαντι have been combined.

6   Changes motivated by doctrinal and ecclesiastical concerns (Metzger
    & Ehrman, 265-268). A fuller list of passages is given in chapter 17,
    section (e) (pages 103-104).

Mt 1:16   Reference to Joseph as *husband of Mary* changed in
            order to safeguard the doctrine of the virgin birth.

Mk 6:3   Description of Jesus as ὁ τέκτων (*the carpenter*) changed
            to *son of the carpenter*, it being considered not fitting to
            refer to Jesus in such a humble way.

Mk 9:29   *Prayer* changed to *prayer and fasting* in line with the
            common practice of the early church.

Mk 15:34   The concept of God abandoning Jesus on the cross
            might have seemed too difficult to a scribe who
            changed *why have you forsaken me?* (ἐγκαταλείπω) to *why
            have you reproached me?* (ὀνειδίζω).

Acts 20:28 *Church of God* changed to *church of the Lord* because of
            the reference to blood in the next phrase and the
            perceived difficulty of imagining God having blood.

Gal 2:9   Change from *James and Cephas and John* to *Peter and
            James and John*, thus putting Peter at the beginning of
            the list, as may have been thought appropriate.

1 Thess 1:5 *Our gospel* (ie of Paul and others) may have offended
            some scribes who changed it to *the gospel of God* or *the
            gospel of our God*.

2 Tim 3:14 *From whom* (τίνων) *you learned it*, with the plural τίνων
            changed to singular τίνος to make it refer to Paul alone.

1 Pet 5:2   Omission of ἐπισκοποῦντες (*exercising oversight*). If
            understood as describing the role of bishops
            (ἐπίσκοποι), this may have seemed an inappropriate
            command to give to presbyters.

1 Jn 4:3   Change from μὴ ὁμολογεῖ (*does not confess*) to λύει
            (*separates, breaks up*), a polemic against heretics who
            separated the human Jesus and the heavenly Christ.

7   Lectionary or liturgical factors.

Mt 20:31   If ἐλέησον ἡμᾶς, κύριε is original, it could have been
            changed to the more usual liturgical word order κύριε,
            ἐλέησον ἡμᾶς (*Lord, have mercy*).

| Lk 22:31 | Lectionary use is likely to account for the addition of εἶπεν δὲ ὁ κύριος, in order to introduce a reading. |
| Jn 10:22 | Absence of τότε may be explained as an omission due to its redundancy in a liturgical context. |

8   Transposition.

| Mk 10:25 | MS D has placed verse 25 after verse 23, apparently an attempt to improve the logical sequence. |

9   Miscellaneous additions (Metzger & Ehrman, 268-271).

Mt 20:28	Addition at the end of the verse in D and others based on Lk 14:8-10: *But seek to increase from that which is small, and from the greater to become less. When you enter a house and are invited to dine, do not recline in the prominent places, lest perchance one more honorable than you come in, and the host come and say to you, 'Go farther down'; and you will be put to shame. But if you recline in the lower place and one inferior to you comes in, the host will say to you, 'Go farther up'; and this will be advantageous to you.* Described in the *Textual Commentary* (where the Greek text is also given) as a piece of floating tradition, implying that this is not merely a creation of D.
Mk 13:33	In *watch and pray*, the words *and pray* can be regarded as a natural addition, influenced perhaps by 14:38.
Lk 9:54	Addition at the end of the verse: *as Elijah also did.*
Lk 9:55	Addition at the end of the verse: *And he said, 'You do not know of what sort of spirit you are.* Others adding further: *For the son of man did not come to destroy the souls of men but to save.* There are differences in the exact wording of some of these additions.
Lk 16:19	Apparently some felt that the rich man needed to be given a name, including Neves (Νευης), Phinehas, and Amonofis (= Amenophis). There is a long note about this in the *Textual Commentary*.
Lk 24:36	Addition of *It is I, do not be afraid* seems not to be an example of harmonising, but an addition based roughly on Jn 6:20.
Jn 12:1	The description of Lazarus as ὁ τεθνηκώς appears to be an addition.

10   Miscellaneous deletions.

Mk 12:23   The words ὅταν ἀναστῶσιν may have been omitted as a
             clumsy and redundant expression.
Mk 16:1   D has attempted to make several improvements by
             omitting most of the first part of the verse, including
             reference to the passing of the sabbath and the names
             of the women, and simply saying πορευθεῖσαι.
Lk 19:25   D has omitted the verse, possibly as an unnecessary
             interruption to the flow of the passage; perhaps
             influenced by Mt 25:28-29 (harmonisation).

 oooOOOooo

It is recognised that different interpretations can be given for some of these
examples. The comments proceed on the assumption that we know which
reading is earlier and which reading represents a later change. It is also
assumed that we know if a change was accidental or deliberate. However,
needless to say, the scribes have not provided us with notes explaining the
changes they made! Fuller textual analysis is required to decide in each
case which was the earlier reading and which was a later variant.
Nevertheless, these can still serve as illustrations of the sorts of things
which scribes did. Even if a particular example discussed here could be
explained differently, it would not be hard to find other examples to
illustrate the point.

Chapter 8

THE GREEK MANUSCRIPTS

These are the primary resources for the study of the New Testament text. They are traditionally classified under four different headings. The first group are the <u>papyri</u>, which are generally the earliest available sources, none a complete NT and most not even large portions, but usually considered the most valuable of the available evidence. The earliest ($\mathfrak{P}^{52}$) is a fragment of John's Gospel dated to about AD 125. Then there are the <u>uncials</u> or majuscules, so named because of the large (uppercase) letters in which they are written, and distinguished from the papyri by being written on parchment (specially prepared animal skin). Third are the <u>minuscules</u>, likewise on parchment, but written in a smaller cursive script, a style which was developed from the 9th century. Finally there are the <u>lectionaries</u>, not continuous texts of a particular book, but the portions (lections) chosen to be read in church services. This is also the order in which the Greek witnesses are cited in the critical apparatus of the UBS and NA texts.

This classification is not entirely logical, since the first refers to the *material* on which the text was written, the second and third to the *style of writing*, and the fourth to the *context of use*. But these descriptions have become standard and will inevitably continue to be used.

According to the statistics in Metzger & Ehrman (in 2005) there were 116 papyri, 310 uncials, 2,877 minuscules and 2,432 lectionaries which had been catalogued till that point (page 50). Such figures need to be updated for today (2018), but they give a rough idea of how many MSS are extant. These figures are worth comparing with the much smaller numbers of MSS available for many classical works (Greek and Latin), and the much smaller time gap between the earliest MSS and the time of writing. Of course there is a high proportion of later MSS, and it must be remembered that only a few MSS contain the whole NT.

The <u>papyri</u> are referred to by the letter p (or by the Gothic form $\mathfrak{P}$, as we have generally used in this book) with a superscribed number. They are listed and described up to $\mathfrak{P}^{96}$ in Aland, 96-102, with information on content, date, and type of text according to the Alands' five categories (see chapter 6 above; and Aland, 106, 159, 335-336). For the content of the papyri, see also Chart 5 at the end of that book. A fuller description of a select number of the papyri may be found in Metzger & Ehrman, 53-61.

NA[28] (2012) and UBS[5] (2014) list the papyri up to $\mathfrak{P}^{127}$ (with some basic information about each). Of great importance is the information provided by Comfort, who argues that many papyri are earlier than usually regarded. For example he claims that at least twelve papyri should be given a second century date (in contrast to only four in the list in NA[28], namely $\mathfrak{P}^{52}$, $\mathfrak{P}^{90}$, $\mathfrak{P}^{98}$, $\mathfrak{P}^{104}$). He gives detailed comments (with many photographs) about the papyri, arranged chronologically: second century (pages 127-163), first half of the third century (pages 163-187), second half of the third century (pages 187-198). For other information about the papyri, see Comfort, 56-77 and 267-270. It should be acknowledged that not all scholars accept Comfort's views about earlier dating.

The <u>uncials</u> were in earlier times given an alphabetic notation, beginning with א (the Hebrew letter aleph), then the uppercase Roman letters, and finally some of the uppercase Greek letters. There are 37 letters available: the letter aleph, 26 Roman letters, and 10 Greek letters (Γ Δ Θ Λ Ξ Π Σ Φ Ψ Ω). A total of 45 uncials are described this way, with several letters used to describe more than one MS (six are used for two different MSS [D, E, F, G, L, P] and one is used for three [H]). An example of this is MS D, which is used for both Bezae and Claromontanus, but confusion is avoided because Bezae is a MS of the Gospels and Acts and Claromontanus is a Paul MS. Later the uncials were given a numerical notation, with a zero prefixed to each number. Thus א (Sinaiticus) became 01, A (Alexandrinus) became 02, B (Vaticanus) became 03, and so on. The MSS which were described by the same letter were given different numbers (eg Bezae and Claromontanus, which are both D, are numbered 05 and 06 respectively).

The uncials are listed and described up to 0299 in Aland, 107-128, with fuller information about the content of each in Chart 6 at the end of the book. There are about 120 uncials of the 4th-6th century, and only five earlier than these, dating from the beginning of the 4th century or earlier, namely 0162 (3rd/4th), 0171 (about AD 300), 0189 (3rd/4th; this is the date given in Aland, but UBS[5]/NA[28] now date this MS 2nd/3rd), 0212 (3rd) and 0220 (3rd). For all these early uncials, see Aland, 104. A fuller description of a select number of the uncials may be found in Metzger & Ehrman, 62-86; see also Comfort, 77-87.

The <u>minuscules</u> are numbered with simple numerals, from 1 onwards (without a prefixed zero). The most significant minuscules are listed and described in Aland, 129-138. This list includes those with at least some portion of the text *not* of the Byzantine text-type (the latest and least valuable type of text). MSS which are predominantly of the Byzantine text-type are listed in Aland, 138-142 (tables 6 and 7). A fuller description of a select number of the minuscules may be found in Metzger & Ehrman, 86-92; see also Comfort, 87-90.

A useful list of the Greek witnesses (papyri, uncials and minuscules) according to date and the Aland category is given in Aland, 159-162 (table 8). Our editions also contain lists of those used for the preparation of the text: UBS[5], 12*-25*; UBS[4], 7*-18*; NA[28], 792-814.

Lectionaries are described with the letter *l* followed by a superscribed number (*l*[1], *l*[2] etc). The vast majority of the lectionaries represent the standard (late) Byzantine text-type, but for UBS[5] 70 lectionary MSS were identified as having some value for determining the earlier text, according to the statement in UBS[5], 26* (UBS[4], 20*); in fact the UBS lists contain only 69 lectionaries (UBS[5], 28*-29*; UBS[4], 21*-22*). Clearly much more work is needed on the lectionaries (see C.D. Osburn, in Ehrman & Holmes, chapter 4).

The papyri are generally the earliest surviving MSS, though containing only a relatively small amount of text. However, some of the papyri are quite late (some as late as 7th/8th century) and some of the uncials are quite early (some as early as 3rd century), which means that there is considerable overlap in date between papyri and uncials. It is certainly not true that all the papyri are earlier than all the uncials. Similarly, some uncials date from as late as the 10th century, which means that we cannot say that all the minuscules are later than all the uncials; here too there is some overlap in date. The best overview of dating is in Aland, 159-162, which is a chart of all the Greek witnesses arranged century by century.

Chapter 9

OTHER MAJOR EVIDENCE

Versions in other ancient languages

From the second century onwards the need arose to translate NT books into other languages, as the gospel spread to areas where Greek was not the main language or was perhaps not spoken at all. The earlier the translation, the earlier the Greek MSS on which the translation was based. Thus, these translations (known as "versions") can be valuable, though obviously indirect, evidence for the Greek text from which the translation was made. One of the greatest advantages is that a particular version has an obvious geographical location, and this helps to identify the text-type(s) used in different areas of the ancient world.

There are, however, some significant difficulties in using the evidence provided by these versions. Even the earliest of the versions are too late to be of much use in establishing the *original* NT text. Furthermore, it is far from simple to work back from the text we find in another language to the Greek from which the version was translated, especially when there are important differences in the grammatical structure of Greek and the target language. At the same time, the problem of back-translation should not be exaggerated, for in most cases scholars do not have to *guess* what the Greek text might have been since the options are already defined by the variants available in the Greek MSS.

The earliest and most significant of the translations are the Syriac and Latin. Others are the Coptic, Ethiopic, Armenian, Georgian and Slavonic. These are described in Metzger & Ehrman, 94-126; Aland, 185-214; Comfort, 91-97. More comprehensive surveys of these different versions and the challenges which scholars face in putting their evidence to good use in textual criticism are contained in Metzger, *The Early Versions of the New Testament*, and in Ehrman & Holmes, chapters 5-11.

Patristic evidence

The early Christian writers (known as the Fathers, and hence the word "patristic") naturally made use of NT passages, sometimes by means of direct quotations and sometimes through allusions to a text. Of most importance are quotations in Greek writers, but Latin and Syriac authors have also produced some valuable evidence.

The patristic evidence enables text critics to locate particular forms of the text to specific geographical areas (as with the versions) and to specific dates. And the fact that the evidence is in Greek (at least for the Greek Fathers) means that the problem of translation back from a different language does not arise.

Nevertheless major obstacles remain in making use of this evidence. These include the difficulty of knowing whether the Father is copying a passage from a MS or quoting from memory or not intending to quote but merely to give the approximate words of a passage. Some Fathers normally cite biblical texts with accuracy and care but others can be quite careless. There is also the challenge of identifying whether and to what extent the text of the Father has itself been changed by the scribes who copied it so as to bring biblical citations into line with a form more familiar to the scribe.

The problems are increased when we consider biblical references in Latin and Syriac writers, in which the problem of the Greek original also becomes part of the equation.

But on a more positive note, the potential value of the evidence of the Fathers may be seen in the following concluding sentences of an article by G.D. Fee (in Epp & Fee, 358-359):

> It is now certain that two distinct forms of the NT existed in the East and West. The last authors in the West to write in Greek (Hippolytus of Rome and Irenaeus of Lyons) both used Greek texts that looked very much like those that lay behind the earliest Latin versions. Tertullian, and all subsequent writers in Latin, are clearly dependent on these Latin versions.
>
> A different picture emerges in Egypt, where the basic text, such as that found in Origen and the earliest Greek MSS from this area (P^{75} P^{46} P^{72} B, and to a lesser degree P^{66}), looks very much like a good, but not perfect, preservation of the original texts themselves. When Origen moved to Caesarea (230 CE) he appears to have taken along his Alexandrian copy of John's Gospel; however, for much of the rest of the NT he began to use texts that differed considerably from those in Alexandria. Similar, somewhat mixed texts can also be found in other early writers from this area (e.g., Eusebius, Epiphanius, Cyril of Jerusalem, Basil). In the meantime the later writers in Alexandria (Didymus, Cyril) exhibit texts that have begun to be modified toward a text that emerges about the same time in Antioch and elsewhere. The earliest Father with extant text,

who used this emerging text, is Asterius the Sophist. This text was also that used by Chrysostom in Antioch and then in Constantinople; although it looked very much like Basil's, it had been modified considerably, so that it was about seventy-five percent along the way to the text that would eventually dominate in the Greek church – probably very much under the influence of Chrysostom himself.

Even if you do not understand all the details in this quotation, you may be able to begin to see how study of NT quotations in the Fathers gives a picture of how the text developed in different places in the early centuries.

Further information about the value and use of the Fathers in textual criticism is given in Metzger & Ehrman, 126-134, and in Aland, 171-184 (Greek Fathers) and 214-221 (Latin and Eastern Fathers). The lists of the Fathers in Aland contain more descriptive information than the UBS lists. The Greek, Latin and Syriac Fathers are discussed in Ehrman & Holmes, chapters 12-14. Our editions contain lists of the Fathers used for the preparation of the text: UBS[5], 38*-43*; UBS[4], 32*-37*; NA[28], 80*-81*.

Chapter 10

USING THE UBS EDITION

In this chapter we are not attempting to evaluate the variants but simply to practise reading the textual notes (the apparatus) of UBS. How does this commonly used text record the witnesses to the variant readings? The following notes are based on UBS[5]. Any difference in detail in UBS[4] is noted.

Before we look at some examples, we note several features of UBS. Many (though not all) pages of UBS contain three apparatus sections. The first is the main apparatus, containing the variant readings and the evidence for each. Near the beginning of each apparatus unit, we find a rating for the reading of the text. This system is explained in the introduction (UBS[5], 8*-9*; UBS[4], 3*): {A} indicates that the text is certain, {B} indicates that the text is almost certain, {C} indicates that the Committee had difficulty in deciding which variant to place in the text, {D} indicates that the Committee had great difficulty in arriving at a decision.

The second section of the apparatus of UBS on each page indicates the different punctuations used for a particular passage in other editions of the Greek NT as well as in selected translations. This is called the Discourse Segmentation Apparatus and is explained in the introduction (UBS[5], 51*-56*; UBS[4], 40*-46*).

The third section of the apparatus of UBS on each page contains selected cross references. See the introduction (UBS[5], 56*-58*; UBS[4], 46*-47*).

Mark 1:1

At the end of the verse we see the superscribed number "1", indicating a note in the textual apparatus. So we look in the apparatus for note 1 for verse 1, which we find indicated in the form [1] **1**.

Immediately after [1] **1** comes {C}, meaning that the editors had difficulty in deciding which variant to place in the text (page 8*; UBS[4], 3*). Then the different readings are given, with the evidence in support of each. The evidence is presented in the order Greek witnesses (papyri, uncials, minuscules, lectionaries), versions, and patristic authors. Information about these witnesses is provided in the UBS introduction (pages 12*-46*; UBS[4], 7*-37*). Parallel lines // mark the end of the evidence for each reading.

Finding the New Testament

First option (the reading of the text): Χριστοῦ υἱοῦ θεοῦ

1   Greek witnesses
    a   Papyri   None
    b   Uncials   אֹ¹ B D L W. אֹ¹ the first corrector of this MS; the original scribe of אֹ is recorded as אֹ*, as in the fourth option below (page 25*; UBS⁴, 19*). For the date of the correctors of some of the main uncials, see the end of appendix 1 (page 118).
    c   Minuscules   2427. This is in UBS⁴ but not in UBS⁵; it is one of the minuscules *not* used for UBS⁵; see chapter 11.
    d   Lectionaries None

2   Versions: no versions

3   Patristic evidence: no patristic evidence

Second option: Χριστοῦ υἱοῦ τοῦ θεοῦ

1   Greek witnesses
    a   Papyri   None
    b   Uncials   A Δ
    c   Minuscules   *f*¹ *f*¹³ 33 180 205 565 579 597 700 892 1006 1010 1071 1243 1292 1342 1424 1505 *Byz*. *f*¹ means MS 1 and other minuscules which belong to the same family of MSS (page 25*; UBS⁴, 18*); *f*¹³ means MS 13 and other minuscules which belong to the same family of MSS (page 25*; UBS⁴, 19*). *Byz* means the Byzantine witnesses in general (page 25*; UBS⁴, 19*). E F G H Σ in square brackets after *Byz* are of course uncials, not minuscules, but it is convenient to list them here because they are important Byzantine MSS (pages 10*, 25*; UBS⁴, 4*, 19*). The abbreviation supp in Gˢᵘᵖᵖ is defined as a reading "*supplied* by a later hand where the original is missing, usually representing a different text-type" (page 26*; UBS⁴, 20*).
    d   Lectionaries *Lect* (page 29*; UBS⁴ page 22*) means the majority of the lectionaries listed on pages 28*-29* (UBS⁴, 21*-22*).

2   Versions
    a   Ethiopic   eth indicates the Ethiopic tradition in general. Individual editions of the Ethiopic text are listed on page 35* (UBS[4], 29*).
    b   Georgian   geo[2] is a revision of the Georgian tradition (page 35*; UBS[4], 28*-29*).
    c   Slavonic   slav is the Old Church Slavonic version (page 36*; UBS[4], 29*).

3   Other evidence. There are two more lines of information enclosed in brackets. Evidence is provided for either υἱοῦ θεοῦ (the first option) or υἱοῦ τοῦ θεοῦ (the second option). The languages of the witnesses listed here do not have a definite article, and so there is no way of knowing whether the Greek exemplar from which the translation has been made contained τοῦ or did not contain τοῦ. Evidence of two types is given, first from some versions and then from some Fathers:

    a   Versions. Latin: ten Old Latin MSS (it[a], etc) (pages 31*-33*; UBS[4], 24*-26*) and the Vulgate Latin version (vg) (page 33*; UBS[4], 27*). Syriac: different forms of the Syriac version (syr[p, h]) (page 34*; UBS[4], 27*-28*). Coptic: different forms of the Coptic version (cop[sa mss, bo]) (pages 34*-35*; UBS[4], 28*); the superscribed "mss" with "cop[sa]" means some MSS of the Coptic Sahidic version.
    b   Fathers. These are all Latin texts. Usually the Greek Fathers are listed first and then the Latin Fathers, following a semi-colon. Here we have a semi-colon after Irenaeus (because he is included in the list of Greek Fathers on page 40* [UBS[4], 33*]). The Greek Fathers are always listed first, even when (as here) it is a Latin translation of a Father's work which is cited. Irenaeus[lat 2/3] means two of the three times when the Latin text of Irenaeus quotes this passage. Also Jerome[3/6] means three of the six times Jerome quotes this passage.

Third option: Χριστοῦ υἱοῦ τοῦ κυρίου

One Greek witness alone contains this reading, the minuscule 1241.

Fourth option: Χριστοῦ

1   Greek witnesses
    a   Papyri   None
    b   Uncials   א* Θ

c   Minuscules   28ᶜ. This means a corrected form of 28 (page 25*; UBS⁴, 19*).

d   Lectionaries   None

2   Versions: Four versions are mentioned. syrᵖᵃˡ is a form of the Syriac version (page 34*; UBS⁴, 27*-28*), copˢᵃ ᵐˢ means one MS of the Coptic Sahidic version (pages 34*-35*; UBS⁴, 28*), arm is the Armenian trad-ition, geo¹ is a revision of the Georgian tradition (page 35*; UBS⁴, 29*).

3   Patristic evidence. Several Greek Fathers are mentioned, then (starting with Victorinus-Pettau) some Latin Fathers. Rather than print Origen twice (once for his Greek text, once for his Latin text), he is given simply as Origenᵍʳ· ˡᵃᵗ. Jerome³/⁶ means three of the six times Jerome quotes this passage.

Fifth option: *omit*. This means that the words of the first option (Χριστοῦ υἱοῦ θεοῦ) are omitted completely.

1   Greek witnesses. One Greek minuscule 28* contains this reading. The asterisk means the original of 28, in contrast to 28ᶜ which has the fourth option. Originally 28 did not have the three words but a later scribe did not like this and added Χριστοῦ.

2   Patristic evidence. Irenaeusᵍʳ· ˡᵃᵗ ¹/³ means Irenaeus' Greek text, plus one of the three times this passage is quoted in the Latin version of Irenaeus. This evidence from Irenaeus and Epiphanius is enclosed in brackets. Brackets indicate "a *negligible* difference in the witness to the reading attested" (page 25*; UBS⁴, 19*). In this particular case, the extra difference is explained at the end of the note, which is that the word Ἰησοῦ is also omitted. What this means is that in these witnesses the text of Mark 1:1 is simply ἀρχὴ τοῦ εὐαγγελίου. This *could* have been given as a sixth option, if the editors had chosen to do so.

A comment may be made about the use of *square brackets*, as at the end of Mark 1:1. It is explained (page 7*, UBS⁴, 2*) that this indicates words which may be regarded as part of the text but not with complete certainty, and that the bracketed words have a {C} rating. No apparatus note is provided for variants of minor grammatical significance or minor significance to translation, but where there is an apparatus note (as here) it is not clear that the brackets provide any information which is not already available.

John 1:18

After θεός the superscribed number "5" leads us to look in the apparatus for note 5 for verse 18, which we find indicated in the form ⁵ **18**.

Immediately after ⁵ **18** comes {B}, meaning that the text is almost certain, in the opinion of the editors (page 8*; UBS⁴, 3*). Then the evidence is presented for each possible reading, in the same order as we have already seen. In the following notes explanations given in the previous example are not repeated.

First option (the reading of the text): μονογενὴς θεός

1   Greek witnesses
   a   Papyri   𝔓⁶⁶
   b   Uncials   א* B C* L
   c   Minuscules   None
   d   Lectionaries   None

2   Versions: part of the Syriac and Georgian traditions.

3   Patristic evidence: the Greek Fathers Origen, Didymus and Cyril, in the case of Origen and Cyril only in part. Cyril mentioned alone means Cyril of Alexandria, in contrast to Cyril-Jerusalem which means Cyril of Jerusalem (page 39*; UBS⁴, 33*)

Second option: ὁ μονογενὴς θεός

1   Greek witnesses
   a   Papyri   𝔓⁷⁵
   b   Uncials   א², meaning the second corrector of א
   c   Minuscules   33
   d   Lectionaries   None

2   Versions: part of the Coptic tradition.

3   Patristic evidence: several Greek Fathers are cited. Several attest this option only in some of their work (eg Eusebius³ᐟ⁷). Clement means Clement of Alexandria (not Clement of Rome, who does not quote any NT texts), and Clement^from Theodotus refers to a work by Clement called *Excerpta ex Theodoto* (page 39*; UBS⁴, 33*).

<u>Third option</u>: ὁ μονογενὴς υἱός

1   Greek witnesses
     a   Papyri   None
     b   Uncials   A C³ W^supp Δ Θ Ψ 0141. C³ means the third
                          corrector of this MS.
     c   Minuscules   *f*¹ *f*¹³ 28 157 180 205 565 579 597 700 892 1006 1010
                          1071 1241 1243 1292 1342 1424 1505 *Byz* [E F G H]
     d   Lectionaries   *Lect* means the majority of the lectionary tradition.

2   Versions. Several different languages are included in the list of
     witnesses here: Latin (it = Old Latin, and vg = Vulgate), Syriac,
     Armenian, Ethiopic, Georgian and Slavonic.

3   Patristic evidence. There is a long list of Greek and Latin Fathers
     (Tertullian being the first of the Latin).

At the end of the evidence for this option we see REB (Revised English
Bible) and BJ (La Bible de Jérusalem). This means that this option has been
preferred as the basis of translation in these Bibles. This is explained on
page 2* (with a full list of the modern editions on page 56*). This
information is new in UBS⁵, and is not in UBS⁴ at all.

<u>Fourth option</u>: μονογενὴς υἱὸς θεοῦ

This reading is found in only one Old Latin MS (it^q) and in some texts of
the Fathers. The abbreviation vid (in Ambrose^{1/11vid}) means "the *most
probable* reading of a manuscript where the state of its preservation makes
complete verification impossible" (page 26*; UBS⁴, 20*). vid stands for the
Latin word *videtur*, meaning *it appears*.

<u>Fifth option</u>: ὁ μονογενής

For this option there is only one Vulgate MS (which is the meaning of vg^ms),
and one time out of two where the passage is quoted by a writer of IV/V
century, known as Pseudo-Vigilius (Ps-Vigilius^{1/2}).

oooOOOooo

By now you will be aware that the apparatus uses many symbols and
abbreviations. Many of these are used frequently and you will soon
become familiar with them. Others are seen only rarely. A useful master
list of these is provided in UBS⁵, 58*-63* or UBS⁴, 48*-53*.

Chapter 11

DISTINCTIVES OF THE
UBS 5th EDITION

At the time of publication of this book (2018), it is likely that some students will still be using the 4th edition of UBS. For the main purposes of this subject, UBS⁴ is quite adequate, but now that UBS⁵ has been published and will increasingly be used, it is important that some brief comments be made about it. In this chapter we draw attention to differences between UBS⁴ and UBS⁵, and also make some observations on the presentation of the text and the apparatus.

It has already been observed that the 2014 edition of UBS is the first since 1975 (nearly 40 years) to be printed with any differences in the text. Nearly all of these occur in the catholic epistles (James - Jude). The differences in the catholic epistles are listed in appendix 3 of this book. However, there are other points of difference which we can note.

Differences in the MSS cited in UBS⁴ and UBS⁵

Many of these are related to the catholic epistles, where work for the *Editio Critica Maior* (mentioned at the end of chapter 5) has led to fresh assessments of the value of certain MSS, particularly though not only among the minuscules, and the result has been that some have been excluded from consideration for UBS⁵ (and so are omitted from the apparatus) and others not previously taken into account have been added. The omitted MSS are now not considered to be sufficiently distinctive for the purpose of textual criticism. But the differences are not only related to the catholic epistles. For example, there are eleven recently-edited papyrus pieces, only one of which ($\mathfrak{P}^{125}$) has text of the catholic epistles.

MSS used in UBS⁴ but omitted in UBS⁵

Uncials	0156 0173 0206 0232 0245 0246 0247 0251
Minuscules	322 323 1067 1846 2138 2298 2427

MSS not used in UBS[4] but added in UBS[5]

Papyri $\mathfrak{P}^{117}$ $\mathfrak{P}^{118}$ $\mathfrak{P}^{119}$ $\mathfrak{P}^{120}$ $\mathfrak{P}^{121}$ $\mathfrak{P}^{122}$ $\mathfrak{P}^{123}$ $\mathfrak{P}^{124}$ $\mathfrak{P}^{125}$ $\mathfrak{P}^{126}$ $\mathfrak{P}^{127}$
Uncials   M (021) S (028) X (033) Γ (036) Λ (039) Π (041) Φ (043)
              047
Minuscules   5 88 221 225 249 429 442 629 636 642 918 1253 1333
              1448 2318 2473 2492

UBS[4] and UBS[5] outside the catholic epistles

There is not much to note here. There seem to be no differences in the variants recorded or the rating assigned to the chosen text, and only minor differences in the textual information provided (see above for the MSS omitted or added in UBS[5]). In these NT books, no variants included in the apparatus of UBS[4] have been omitted, and no new variants have been included in the apparatus of UBS[5].

Apart from MSS now included or omitted (as explained above), the main change in the textual apparatus of UBS[5] is the addition of information regarding the textual basis for several modern translations. The English versions considered are GNB (1992), NIV (1984), NRSV (1989) and REB (1989). This is for situations where a modern translation is based on a reading *other than* the one preferred by the UBS[5] editors. This is explained in the UBS[5] introduction (pages 46*-51*). This is useful information about Bible translation, but it is not strictly *textual* information. However, it does provide a picture of how other scholars involved in translation projects have sometimes disagreed with the editors of UBS[5].

There are a very few minor typographical changes in these books:

Luke 24:6. In UBS[4] the text is printed ἀλλὰ ἠγέρθη with the apparatus reading ἀλλὰ (or ἀλλ᾽) ἠγέρθη. In UBS[5] (text and apparatus) it is ἀλλ᾽ ἠγέρθη with no indication that ἀλλά appears in any MS.
John 7:10. The same comment regarding ἀλλά as for Luke 24:6. In UBS[4] ἀλλὰ [ὡς]; in UBS[5] ἀλλ᾽ [ὡς].
Rev 22:14. The rating in the apparatus for the relevant passage is {A} in UBS[4] but no rating has been given in the UBS[5] apparatus. There is no obvious reason for this omission, which appears to be accidental.

The text of UBS[5] in the catholic epistles (James - Jude)

There are 34 passages where the main text of UBS[5] (in line with NA[28] and *ECM*) differs from UBS[4]. These are listed in UBS[5], 3*-4* (where for unknown reasons 1 Peter 2:25 is omitted) and in appendix 3 of this book. Clearly this is not a large quantity. The catholic epistles occupy 55 pages in UBS[5], so 34 changes amount to one change per 1.6 pages. Thus the new edition can hardly be seen as a radically different text.

However, one factor suggests a greater degree of uncertainty about the text. A diamond is used to identify passages about which "the highest level of uncertainty" attaches to a textual decision (UBS[5], 9*). There are 42 such passages: 32 are listed in UBS[5], 890 (passages for which no apparatus unit is provided), and there are ten others for which there is an apparatus unit. None of these is given a rating, in contrast to the normal rating system in the UBS editions, but the description "the highest level of uncertainty" implies a {D} rating for these 42 passages. This indicates much less certainty about the text than in UBS[3], which has 15 {D} rated passages in the catholic epistles, and in UBS[4], which has only two {D} rated passages, both of which ironically have been upgraded to {C} in UBS[5].

To express this same point in a different way, there are 178 passages (in the catholic epistles) in UBS[5] where variants are attested: 129 passages where there is an apparatus unit, and 49 where there is no apparatus unit. These 49 consist of 20 of the passages listed in UBS[5], 3*-4*, and 29 of the 32 passages listed in UBS[5], 890 (three of that list are already included on pages 3*-4*, ie 1 Pet 5:9, 1 Jn 1:7, Jude 18, and are not included twice in the count). This total number (178) is much higher than the 143 variants indicated in UBS[4]: 137 passages where there is an apparatus unit, plus six others where there is no apparatus unit but where the use of square brackets in the UBS[4] text indicates the existence of a variant.

To summarise, there are few substantial changes in the actual text, but much greater evidence of overall uncertainty on the part of the editors.

The apparatus of UBS[5] in the catholic epistles (James - Jude)

There are several unsatisfactory aspects of the apparatus of UBS[5]:

(a) Use of the diamond. We have already noticed this feature to mark uncertain passages in 42 places. For 32 of these (listed in UBS[5], 890) no apparatus unit is provided, despite the fact that in three of these (James 4:14, 1 Pet 5:11, 2 Pet 1:5) UBS[4] does have an apparatus unit. There are a further 10 for which UBS⁵ does include an apparatus unit (James 5:4, 1 Pet 1:22, 5:10, 2 Pet 1:4, 2:11, 1 Jn 1:4, 2:6, 4:20, 5:6, 2 Jn 12). The justification for the passages listed on page 890 *not* being given an apparatus unit is that the variants are of no relevance for translation and exegesis (UBS⁵, 4*), but surely that is not so in several examples, such as 1 Pet 2:12 (ἐποπτεύοντες present, and ἐποπτεύσαντες aorist), 2 Pet 2:3 (νυστάζει present, and νυστάξει future), 1 Jn 2:29 (εἰδῆτε *know*, and ἴδητε *see*) and 2 Jn 9 (reversed order of *Father* and *Son*). As it stands, the use of the diamond is potentially confusing. For passages which have "the highest level of uncertainty", a better approach might be to use the diamond for one purpose only, that is, for passages that have variants without relevance for translation or exegesis, to choose such passages with more discrimination, and to place these in an appendix. For other such uncertain passages (those considered relevant for translation and exegesis) for which an apparatus unit needs to be provided, forget the diamond and simply give a {D} rating.

(b) Treatment of the 34 changed passages. Twenty-one of these are printed without an apparatus unit; that is, for about 60% of examples no justification is provided for the change in text nor even an indication in the body of the edition that variants exist. Perhaps (as with some of the diamond-marked passages just mentioned) it was considered that these 21 passages are not significant for translation and exegesis. Nevertheless, it seems strange that the editors go to some trouble to draw attention to the changes that have been made without feeling that the reader is entitled to be given some evidence to support each change.

(c) Other passages without an apparatus unit. There are nine other passages where the text of UBS⁵ is printed without comment (thus implying an {A} rating) in contrast to a {C} rating in UBS⁴. In six of these, square brackets in the UBS⁴ text indicate a variant and imply a {C} rating for the chosen text (1 Pet 1:6, 3:22, 4:17, 5:5, 2 Pet 3:3, 1 Jn 5:5), and there are three others for which UBS⁴ has an apparatus unit and a {C} rating for the chosen text (1 Pet 1:12, 3:1, 1 Jn 5:1). Without an apparatus unit for any of these passages in UBS⁵, it is impossible to evaluate the basis for the editors' increased confidence regarding the text they have printed.

oooOOOooo

The preceding comments draw attention to several aspects which may be considered peculiarities of UBS⁵, and which are potentially confusing to the user. It is clear that the ongoing publication of the *ECM* will mean many changes in future editions of UBS in other parts of the NT as well as the catholic epistles, and it may be hoped that the presentation of the text and apparatus of future editions will avoid some of these issues.

Chapter 12

INTRODUCING NESTLE-ALAND

Though this course is based on the UBS edition, it is important for students to have a basic understanding of Nestle-Aland as well. We need to learn how to read the NA apparatus and to be aware of the differences between UBS and NA.

Leaving aside the text itself, which apart from some variations in punctuation and other minor matters is the same as in UBS, these are the main differences between UBS and NA:

1   NA records more variants than UBS. UBS is intended in the first place for the use of Bible translators and so its variants are limited to those which are claimed to have a direct effect on translation.
2   The recording of the variants in the apparatus is done differently. UBS prints all variants in full, whereas NA uses a system of symbols and abbreviations (as explained below).
3   UBS gives the witnesses for each variant in a much fuller form than does NA.
4   NA does not use the UBS rating system.
5   NA does not have the Discourse Segmentation Apparatus which we find in UBS.
6   Instead of UBS's cross reference system (the third section of the UBS apparatus), NA has a much fuller system of cross references in the outer margin of each page adjacent to the relevant part of the text.
7   In the inner margin of each page of the four Gospels, NA has a set of notations which record the Eusebian canons, an ancient system of finding parallel passages in the other Gospels. The tables for these are found in NA[28], 90*-94*, and the system is explained in Metzger & Ehrman, 38-39.

Most of these differences mean that UBS is in many ways easier to use and more useful for Bible translators, but the much higher number of variants recorded in NA means that it is a better edition for someone with a serious interest in textual criticism.

NA sets out the textual witnesses in the same way as UBS. First, the Greek witnesses are given, in the order papyri, uncials, minuscules, lectionaries (only five lectionaries are used, as listed at the end of the Greek witnesses in NA[28], 814). Then comes the evidence of the versions. Finally, the patristic witnesses are listed, with names printed in full (UBS) or in abbreviated form (NA).

As mentioned above, NA uses symbols and abbreviations to refer to variants. A variant is identified in the main text in the following ways:

1   ⊤ means that there is something added at this point (one or more words) in some witnesses.
2   ° means that the following word is omitted in some witnesses.
3   ⊐ ヽ means that the words between these two symbols are omitted in some witnesses.
4   ⌐ means that there is an alternative to the following word in some witnesses.
5   ⸌ ⸍ means that there is an alternative to the words between these two symbols in some witnesses.
6   ⸉ ⸊ means that there is a transposition (ie a change of word order) of the words between these two symbols in some witnesses.

The same symbols are used in the apparatus to identify the reading in the text for which there are one or more variants (except that, where there are two symbols [points 3, 5 and 6 above], only the first is used in the apparatus, ie ⊐ alone, not ⊐ ヽ; ⸌ alone, not ⸌ ⸍; and ⸉ alone, not ⸉ ⸊). In the apparatus the relevant Greek words of the variant(s) are abbreviated whenever possible. The names of the Fathers are also abbreviated. It takes a little while to become familiar with this system, but once you are familiar with it, it is quite straightforward to use, and means that a large amount of information can be presented in a relatively small space.

Here are some examples of each of these types of variants, from the early chapters of John's Gospel:

1   In John 1:15 the text reads ὁ ὀπίσω μου ἐρχόμενος ⊤ ἔμπροσθέν μου γέγονεν. This means that some witnesses have an addition between ἐρχόμενος and ἔμπροσθεν. By looking in the apparatus for the symbol ⊤ for this verse, you can see that ὅς is added at this point in some witnesses.

2   In John 1:21 the text reads ° καὶ λέγει. This means that some witnesses omit the word καί. In the apparatus we simply find the symbol ° followed by a list of the witnesses for the omission of this word.

3   In John 1:4 the text reads τὸ φῶς ⊐ τῶν ἀνθρώπων ヽ . This means that some witnesses omit the words τῶν ἀνθρώπων. In the apparatus the symbol ⊐ alone introduces the relevant information about the variant.

4   In John 1:6 the text reads παρὰ ⌐ θεοῦ. This means that some witnesses replace the word θεοῦ with something different. By looking in the apparatus for the symbol ⌐ , one can see that the word κυρίου is used at this point in one witness.

5   In John 1:15 the text (NA²⁷) reads ⌐ οὗτος ἦν ὃν εἶπον ⌐. This means that some witnesses replace these words with something different. By looking in the apparatus for the symbol ⌐ , one finds two other readings for this passage: some witnesses have ουτ. ην ο ειπων, and one other witness has ουτ. ην. The apparatus presents these variants in abbreviated form (that is, abbreviated spelling and without accents or breathing marks). It is expected that the reader has the ability to work out the full form, either because some of the words are the same as in the text or through general knowledge of Greek grammar. Thus, in these examples the full forms of the two variants are οὗτος ἦν ὁ εἰπών and οὗτος ἦν.

At this point NA²⁸ presents the same information in a slightly different form to NA²⁷. The text of NA²⁸ has οὗτος ἦν ⌐ ὃν εἶπον ⌐ instead of ⌐ οὗτος ἦν ὃν εἶπον ⌐, and the apparatus says that instead of ὃν εἶπον some witnesses have ο ειπων, and one other witness omits the two words. The final result is the same as in NA²⁷; that is, the readings under consideration are οὗτος ἦν ὃν εἶπον (the reading of the text), and the two in the apparatus οὗτος ἦν ὁ εἰπών and οὗτος ἦν.

6   In John 1:28 the text reads ⌐ ἐν ⌐ Βηθανίᾳ ἐγένετο ⌐. Here two different variants are involved. The symbols ⌐ ⌐ indicate a transposition, and in the apparatus one finds the symbol ⌐ followed by a list of witnesses in support of the transposition. Here there are three Greek words (which can be numbered 1 2 3). In other examples of transposition the apparatus specifically indicates the order; if that had been done here, the apparatus would have contained the numbers 3 1 2 (to show the order of these three words in the variant). But in this passage this has not been done, because only one transposition is possible: the only two possibilities are ἐν Βηθανίᾳ ἐγένετο (the text) and ἐγένετο ἐν Βηθανίᾳ (the transposed order of the variant). (In 2:10, the text has ⌐ πρῶτον τὸν καλὸν οἶνον ⌐. The apparatus indicates that the variant has the order 2-4 1, meaning that the actual variant is τὸν καλὸν οἶνον πρῶτον.)

The other variant in 1:28 concerns the word Βηθανίᾳ. The symbol ⌐ means that this is replaced by something different in some witnesses. The apparatus reveals that there are two alternatives: Βηθαβαρα and

Βηθαραβα. As elsewhere these variants are not given in full. Here the accents and iota subscript have been omitted.

To illustrate further the differences between UBS and NA, here is NA's treatment of the same variant in John 1:18 which we used in chapter 10 to illustrate UBS's apparatus.

The relevant words in the text are printed as ⸆ μονογενὴς θεὸς ⸇ . The symbols used here mean that some witnesses replace these words with something different (page 60, point 5). The NA apparatus is:

18 ⸆ ο μονογενης θεος 𝔓[75] 𝑥[1] 33; Cl[pt] Cl[ex Thd pt] Or[pt] ¦ ο μονογενης υιος A C[3] K Γ Δ Θ Ψ *f*[1.13] 565. 579. 700. 892. 1241. 1424 𝔐 lat sy[c.h]; Cl[pt] Cl[ex Thd pt] Or[pt] ¦ ει μη ο μονογενης υιος W[s] it; Ir[lat pt] (+ θεου Ir[lat pt]) ¦ *txt* 𝔓[66] 𝑥* B C* L sy[p.hmg]; Or[pt] Did |

When we compare this to the UBS apparatus for the same passage, we notice the following points:

1   The division between variants is marked ¦ , rather than ∥ , and the end of the apparatus unit is marked by a single solid line, that is | .
2   The reading of the text (marked as *txt*) is recorded at the *end* of the apparatus unit rather than the beginning.
3   Different options are recorded: four in NA, five in UBS. NA's third does not appear in UBS, and the last two in UBS are not included in NA. This reveals the editors' choice, based on their evaluation of the significance of particular variants.
4   The presentation of data follows the same order as in UBS: Greek witnesses, versions and Fathers, lectionaries.
5   The witnesses for each variant are similar to what we see in UBS but not identical. This also represents the editors' choice regarding what they consider to be significant witnesses.
6   The symbols used are also similar but not identical. 𝔐 (Majority text) is essentially the same as *Byz* in UBS. Fathers are abbreviated, eg Ir for Irenaeus, Or for Origen, Cl for Clement of Alexandria.

These points mean that the NA apparatus certainly looks different from UBS, but with practice it is easy enough to use.

Whether you are using UBS[4] or UBS[5], or NA[27] or NA[28], it is important to read carefully and refer continually to the explanations in the introduction to your edition. Lengthy explanations may be found in Aland, 224-232, for UBS[4], and in Aland, 232-260, for NA[27], most of which applies also to UBS[5] and NA[28].

Chapter 13

CRITERIA FOR TEXTUAL DECISIONS

Quite early in the story of textual criticism scholars started to identify possible criteria for deciding the reading likely to be original or at least the earliest available to us (chapter 2). In discussing eclecticism (chapter 6) we saw that there are several criteria which need to be taken into account, divided into external and internal criteria. We now need to look at these more fully. After listing the criteria given by different scholars, we will make some comments, especially about the external criteria.

The main criteria

Here is a list of criteria is based on the description in Metzger & Ehrman, 302-304, though not all of their points are reproduced here.

A   External Criteria

1   The date of the witness and especially of the type of text which it contains. (A MS may have been copied in the 6th century, but if it can be demonstrated that it is based on a much earlier MS, it is the earlier date which is most relevant.)

2   The geographical location of a witness. Where was the MS produced? If a variant is found in witnesses from several different geographical locations, this increases the likelihood of that variant being original.

3   The relationship of a MS to other MSS. Much work has been done to try to group the MSS. It is obvious that if twenty MSS were copied from the one MS, there are not twenty-one separate witnesses but really only one. So MSS must not simply be counted. The original reading is not found by a sort of democratic vote.

B   Internal Criteria

These criteria can be subdivided into two types:

1   Transcriptional probability. These are to do with the habits of *scribes*, and consideration of these habits has produced the following criteria:

a   The more difficult reading is to be preferred to the easier. ("More difficult" means what would have seemed to the scribe to be difficult. A scribe is likely to have changed what seemed to him to be difficult to something more straightforward.)

b   The shorter reading is to be preferred to the longer. (It is considered that scribes had the tendency to include extra material rather than to omit and abbreviate.)

c   The reading which resists the tendency to harmonise is to be preferred.

d   The reading is to be preferred which shows a less familiar Greek word, or has a less refined grammatical form, or avoids the addition of explanatory words and phrases.

2   <u>Intrinsic probability</u>. This is to do with what an *author* was more likely to have written, including the following matters:

a   The author's known style and vocabulary.

b   The immediate context.

c   Harmony with the author's usage elsewhere.

Here are criteria listed by E.J. Epp (in Epp & Fee, chapter 8), summarised from the material on pages 163-164. They are described by Epp as "canons that have survived the test of time".

A   <u>Criteria related to external evidence</u>

1   A variant's support by the earliest MSS, or by MSS assuredly preserving the earliest texts.

2   A variant's support by the "best quality" MSS.

3   A variant's support by MSS with the widest geographical distribution.

4   A variant's support by one or more established groups of MSS of recognized antiquity, character, and perhaps location, that is, of recognized "best quality".

B   <u>Criteria related to internal evidence</u>

1   A variant's status as the shorter or shortest reading.

2   A variant's status as the harder or hardest reading.

3   A variant's fitness to account for the origin, development, or presence of all other readings.

4   A variant's conformity to the author's style and vocabulary.

5   A variant's conformity to the author's theology or ideology.

6   A variant's conformity to Koine (rather than Attic) Greek.

7   A variant's conformity to Semitic forms of expression.
8   A variant's lack of conformity to parallel passages or to extraneous items in its context generally.
9   A variant's lack of conformity to OT passages.
10   A variant's lack of conformity to liturgical forms and usages.
11   A variant's lack of conformity to extrinsic doctrinal views.

A further list of twelve basic criteria is given in Aland, 280-281. If you take the trouble to study these lists and compare them, you will recognise that in spite of differences in detail there are many similarities in the several lists, and in fact a significant measure of agreement. One thing to remember, however, is that some doubts have been expressed about the reliability of the criteria, not least the internal criteria (see chapter 6 in the discussion of eclecticism), and we should be careful not to use any criterion in a rigid way, assuming (for example) that the shorter reading must *always* be the earliest. The criteria can be regarded as useful guidelines but not as infallible rules.

External criteria

(a)   The grouping of MSS

Metzger & Ehrman provide lists of the main witnesses within each text-type (pages 306-313). A similar list is provided in the *Textual Commentary*, 15*-16*. At the same time one must be aware that there are important questions about the text-types. The papyri in particular have shown that the "types" (excluding the Byzantine text) had an early existence, not as distinct editions or recensions, but as separate MSS with relatively loose connections with each other.

The Western text is now regarded more as a group of witnesses that display some common textual tendencies than as a homogeneous text-type. These tendencies include numerous unusual readings, long para-phrase and other additions, harmonising, and substitution of synonyms.

It is now commonly doubted whether there ever was a distinctive Caesarean text. Witnesses previously regarded as Caesarean (especially $\mathfrak{P}^{45}$, W and minuscule families 1 and 13, but also Θ, 28, 565, 700) are now considered to be important individual witnesses roughly midway between the texts represented by B and D rather than representatives of a different text-type. (Although Metzger & Ehrman continue to include the Caesarean group in their fourth edition [pages 310-312], it is not identified as a separate text-type in the *Textual Commentary*, which says: "Although recent research has tended to question the existence of a specifically Caesarean text-type, the individual manuscripts formerly considered to be members of the group remain important witnesses in their own right" [pages 6*-7*].)

The Alexandrian group is much more firmly established, but even here warnings are given that the habit of grouping MSS can tend to obscure distinctive features of the individual MSS which are considered to belong to that group. The same is true even of the Byzantine text-type, which evolved over the centuries before reaching the "Majority Text" form and finally the "Textus Receptus".

(b)   The quality of individual MSS: manuscript mixture

One needs to be constantly aware that a given MS is not necessarily a *consistent* witness to a given text-type. Manuscript mixture is a well-known phenomenon. Thus, the fact that a MS is defined *in general* as an Alexandrian MS or a Western MS does not mean that *all* the readings of that MS are Alexandrian or Western. The Aland categories I, II and III give an idea of the relative mixture from the Byzantine tradition which such MSS may contain. Conversely, a MS which is generally considered Byzantine in its textual character may often preserve readings of a different (earlier) type. Each variant needs to be studied individually. It is not possible, for example, to say absolutely that each and every reading in Vaticanus is automatically an Alexandrian reading.

The problem of manuscript mixture applies especially to the MSS in the Alands' category III. These are sometimes Alexandrian and sometimes Byzantine (possibly also sometimes Western), but how do you decide which one? We may take as an example the 8th century uncial 0250. In the next chapter, we have placed this under the Alexandrian heading for John 8:16 (option 1), because there is clear evidence (eg $\mathfrak{P}^{66}$ $\mathfrak{P}^{75}$ B) that this is an Alexandrian reading. On the other hand, in John 8:38 (second set of variants, option 4) the same MS is placed under the Byzantine heading, because there is no clear evidence that this reading represents any other textual tradition.

The same comment applies to MSS described by Metzger & Ehrman as later Alexandrian or secondary Alexandrian. The later they are, the greater proportion of Byzantine readings they are likely to have, and you will need to exercise discernment to decide whether a particular reading is Alexandrian or Byzantine. For example, in the next chapter, in John 8:57 (option 1) Δ is categorised as Alexandrian because of the clear earlier evidence (eg $\mathfrak{P}^{66}$ B) that its reading here is Alexandrian, whereas in John

8:59 (option 3) it is categorised as Byzantine in the absence of such Alexandrian evidence.

To pursue this point about MS mixture, this applies not only to Byzantine readings found in Alexandrian MSS, but also to Byzantine readings found in Western and Caesarean MSS. Thus, Metzger & Ehrman describe several MSS as Western which the Aland classification shows to be mixed: D (06), G (012), W (in part of Mark) and 614 are category III (probably also the very late 383), and E (08) and F (010) are category II. Likewise, most MSS labelled Caesarean by Metzger & Ehrman are mixed: most are in the Aland category III, including 1 (in the Gospels), 13, 28 (in Mark), 565 and 700; and Θ in category II.

These observations about mixture in MSS suggest that categorising such MSS is not straightforward and that scholars can differ in their final assessment. They arc also are a further reminder that the analysis of the external evidence cannot be done in a mechanical and simplistic way, but the textual character of each variant needs separate analysis.

Nevertheless, even with these qualifications it is still possible to note the text-types in support of each reading. The wider the external support for a reading (in terms of text-types and geographical spread), the more likely it is that such a reading is relatively early.

A basic starting point is the lists of witnesses to the different text-types which are provided in the *Textual Commentary*, 15*-16*, and in Metzger & Ehrman, 306-313. Information about the category allotted by the Alands should also be used, perhaps as redefined earlier for categories I, II and III (Chapter 6). Table 8 in Aland, 159-162, provides a complete list of MSS, arranged chronologically from 2nd century to 16th/17th century and according to the Aland category. Some of the information in these publications is brought together in appendices 1 and 2 of this book. G.D. Fee has provided helpful comments on the text-types in Epp & Fee, chapter 1.

The above comments may seem to make the external evidence impossibly complex to handle. Indeed, it is true that there are complications, and the new student needs to proceed slowly and cautiously, making an effort to understand the reasons for a textual critic's decision in each situation. But in spite of these cautionary comments, the external evidence is regarded as highly significant by most textual critics (the exception being thorough-going eclectics), and with a little practice it is possible to use it helpfully.

Internal criteria

Relevant internal criteria have been occasionally mentioned in earlier chapters, and listed more systematically at the beginning of this chapter. There are many criteria, but they all come under one of these two headings: intrinsic probability (what we consider the author likely to have written), and transcriptional probability (what changes we consider scribes likely to have made). As long as we keep these two broad quest-ions in our mind, we will not go far astray. Through practice we learn which criteria may be relevant in each particular case.

We have also noted previously (page 26) that the reliability of internal criteria is far from a settled matter, despite the fact that these have now been discussed for several centuries. Nevertheless, they are the best we have at present and we must use them. However, we must learn to use them in a discerning manner, recognising that textual criticism is an art as well as a science, which means that we cannot simply apply fixed rules in a mechanical way. Textual criticism is a skill which cannot be learned quickly and easily but must be acquired through experience and practice.

The examples which we will look at in the next three chapters will illustrate some of the important internal criteria which need to be considered when making a textual decision. As we work through these chapters (or some of the examples at least), we can expect to grow in our confidence in using the appropriate criteria.

Chapter 14

INTERPRETING THE VARIANTS OF UBS

We have already had a brief introduction to the various witnesses to the text of the Greek NT (chapters 8 and 9), and to the way this evidence is presented in UBS (chapters 10 and 11) and NA (chapter 12). In chapter 13 we have learned something about the text-critical criteria. Now we need to look more closely at the process of doing textual criticism. What does the information in the textual notes mean, and how can we use the various criteria to interpret it?

For the UBS[4] text the textual decisions are conveniently explained in the *Textual Commentary*, and the editors' opinion about the relative certainty of their decision is shown by the use of the letters A, B, C and D at the beginning of each textual note. It is also helpful to use the *Textual Commentary* to see how the criteria have been utilised by scholars in order to reach their decisions. The comments in the *Textual Commentary* also apply to most of the variants in the UBS[5] apparatus, except where the catholic epistles have a different text.

But we want to go further than the opinion of the editors of the UBS text and to do our own practice at interpreting the textual notes. We also want to go further than the *Textual Commentary*, or at the very least to learn to use this book critically, by asking if we can identify other relevant criteria, or if greater weight should be given to criteria other than those which the *Textual Commentary* has considered important.

We begin by listing each variant separately and clearly, and then for each variant classifying each witness as Alexandrian or Western or "Caesarean" or Byzantine. The data provided in appendix 2 can be used for this, and the following chart provides some general guidelines. Remember that the classification of a mixed MS can change from one passage to another; this point has been explained in the previous chapter.

Alexandrian	Metzger's Alexandrian MSS (including proto-Alexandrian and later-Alexandrian); Aland categories I and II (unless there is contrary information).
Western	Metzger's Western MSS; Aland category IV.
"Caesarean"	Θ 1 (f^1) 13 (f^{13}) 28 565 700. (Also $\mathfrak{P}^{45}$ in the Gospels, and W in Mk 1:1-5:30.)
Byzantine	Metzger's Byzantine MSS; Aland category V.

The main complication is with category III MSS. To repeat what has already been said (pages 68-69), these can be classified as Alexandrian if other witnesses from category I or II (eg 𝔓⁶⁶ 𝔓⁷⁵ B) clearly show that this is an Alexandrian reading. Sometimes they can be classified as Western, for the same sort of reason. Otherwise they should be classified as Byzantine. They are *mixed* MSS, containing readings of different types, and so they are not always classified in the same way.

Remember that witnesses listed as "Caesarean" do not represent a separate text-type. In most cases a "Caesarean" reading will be identified as either Alexandrian or Western. Each example needs to be evaluated separately.

After analysing the external criteria, we then consider the <u>internal criteria</u>. Of the available variants, which is the author more likely to have written (intrinsic probability), and which is/are more likely to be the result of scribal alteration (transcriptional probability). We then weigh up the relevant pieces of information, and come to our decision about the most likely original reading.

For further explanation of this process, see Metzger & Ehrman, 305-315, and for further comment on the use of the criteria (especially the external evidence) see the previous chapter.

Here the evidence of the versions and the Fathers is not referred to in most cases. For the sake of keeping the process simple at this stage of your learning, we are looking only at the Greek witnesses. Sometimes consideration of the versions and Fathers will change the picture slightly, but usually the Greek witnesses are sufficient to give a clear picture of the external evidence for any particular reading.

Variant readings in John 8

The variants considered here are a selection of those included in the UBS apparatus, though not always in the same form as in UBS. For example, in the first passage UBS gives the variants as (1) πατήρ and (2) *omit*. Here we have provided the same information but in a slightly fuller (and hopefully clearer) form. Note that ℵ (though not necessarily its correctors) is Western up to verse 38 and Alexandrian elsewhere.

Verse 16

(1) ὁ πέμψας με πατήρ (*the Father who sent me*)
Alexandrian   𝔓³⁹ 𝔓⁶⁶ 𝔓⁷⁵ ℵ² B L T W Δ Ψ 070 0141 0250 33 157 205 579 892 1071 1241 1243

Western	Though ℵ is Western (in this passage), the same is not necessarily true for ℵ², a 7th century correction.
"Caesarean"	Θ *f*¹ *f*¹³ 28 565 700. In this example these probably provide further support for the Alexandrian reading.
Byzantine	E F G H N 180 597 1006 1010 1292 1342 1424 1505 *Byz Lect.* The Byzantine uncials have been placed in the usual order before the minuscules, rather than in square brackets after *Byz* (as in the apparatus).

(2) ὁ πέμψας με (*he who sent me*)
Western   ℵ* D

For this option there is nothing to put on the Alexandrian, "Caesarean" or Byzantine lines, and so these have been omitted to save space (as in other examples following).

External evidence. The weight and range of evidence clearly favours option 1, which the Latin tradition also (versions and Fathers) shows to be a Western reading. Nevertheless, the combination of ℵ and D for the shorter reading adds a small note of uncertainty.

Internal evidence. πατήρ could be considered secondary, as a scribe may have added the word (as a natural complement) and there is no obvious reason why a scribe would have deliberately omitted it. It is also possible that a scribe accidentally omitted the word, as the omission does not change the meaning of the phrase. Intrinsic probability gives no clear guidance. John's Gospel has multiple examples of both ὁ πέμψας με πατήρ (eg 8:18; also 5:23, 37, 6:44) and ὁ πέμψας με (eg 8:26, 29; also 5:24, 30, 6:38, 39).

The external evidence favours the longer text, but there are also good arguments for the other. The {A} rating of UBS might seem optimistic.

Verse 34

(1) δοῦλός ἐστιν τῆς ἁμαρτίας (*is a slave of sin*)

Alexandrian	𝔓⁶⁶ 𝔓⁷⁵ B C L W Δ Ψ 070 0141 0250 33 157 205 579 892 1071 1243
Western	ℵ
"Caesarean"	Θ *f*¹ *f*¹³ 28 565 700
Byzantine	E F G H N 180 597 1006 1010 1292 1342 1424 1505 *Byz Lect*

(2) δοῦλός ἐστιν (*is a slave*)
Western   D

<u>External evidence</u>. With only D supporting the shorter text (and not much else in the versions or Fathers), the evidence here favours the longer text.

<u>Internal evidence</u>. It is difficult to think of either of these options arising accidentally. If the alteration is deliberate, was a scribe more likely to have omitted τῆς ἁμαρτίας from his exemplar or to have added these words to a shorter earlier text? The omission could be explained on the ground that the scribe considered the meaning to be clear enough without these words, or the addition could be explained on the ground that the scribe considered the words necessary to clarify the meaning.

With the internal evidence ambiguous, external evidence is the deciding factor here, in favour of option 1.

<u>Verse 38</u>

(1) παρὰ τῷ πατρί (*in the presence of the Father*)
   Alexandrian 𝔓⁶⁶ 𝔓⁷⁵ B C L 070

(2) παρὰ τῷ πατρί μου (*in the presence of my Father*)
   Alexandrian Possibly Δ Ψ 0141 0250 157 1071 1243, though without
         early Alexandrian support, these category III witnesses
         are more likely Byzantine.
   Western   ℵ
   "Caesarean" Θ f¹ f¹³ 28 565 700, perhaps to be taken as supporting
         the Western text here.
   Byzantine E F G H N 180 597 1006 1010 1292 1342 1424 1505 *Byz*
         Lect

(3) παρὰ τῷ πατρί μου, ταῦτα
     (*in the presence of my Father, these things I speak*)
   Alexandrian 33 892
   Western   D

(4) ἀπὸ τοῦ πατρός, ταῦτα (*from the Father, these things I speak*)
   Alexandrian W

<u>External evidence</u>. The Alexandrian tradition has preserved three variants, though option 1 is clearly the most strongly supported Alexandrian reading. Options 3 and 4 are found in later Alexandrian witnesses (W 33 892). The Western tradition is also divided, between options 2 and 3. The papyri suggest that option 1 is an earlier reading than option 2.

Internal evidence. Among the four options, there are really only two major differences: the inclusion or omission of μου, and the inclusion or omission of ταῦτα. Both of the longer readings (as in readings 2 and 3) appear to be secondary, as natural expansions for the sake of clarity. The fourth option with ἀπό could also be an attempt to clarify, perhaps with the intention of showing that Jesus' teaching derives *from* the Father, although the phrase ἑώρακα ἀπό is hardly very natural Greek. Perhaps more likely the fourth option is a scribal "error of the mind", an unintentional substitution of ἀπό for παρά. Then there is the issue whether John is more likely to have written *my Father* or *the Father*. We cannot say, because both phrases are commonly used in this Gospel, in this chapter ὁ πατήρ μου in verses 19, 49, 54, and ὁ πατήρ in verse 28.

External and internal factors both suggest the first option to be the earliest of those available to us.

Verse 38

(1) ἠκούσατε παρὰ τοῦ πατρὸς ποιεῖτε (*do what you heard from the Father* - ποιεῖτε is imperative and πατρός refers to God)

   Alexandrian   B L W. 𝔓[75] also supports the text with ἠκούσατε and without ὑμῶν, though with the main verb λαλεῖτε (instead of ποιεῖτε). 597 has preserved an early reading; though Category V (Byzantine), it certainly does not have a Byzantine reading here.

(2) ἠκούσατε παρὰ τοῦ πατρὸς ὑμῶν ποιεῖτε (*you are doing what you heard from your father* - ποιεῖτε is indicative and πατρός refers to the devil)

   Alexandrian   ℵ[2] C 33 892. The lectionaries *l* [524] *l* [547], usually regarded as Byzantine, here preserve an early reading. 0141 also testifies to this reading, except for the dative τῷ πατρί instead of the genitive. ℵ[2] is a 7th century corrector of ℵ, here preserving an Alexandrian reading.

   "Caesarean"   Θ *f* [13] 1 565. Perhaps Alexandrian here. If minuscule 1 is cited alone (as here), it means that it does not agree with the other members of family 1 (*f* [1]); the other MSS in this family have a different reading here. Similarly with minuscule 13 (see verse 39, option 1).

(3) ἑωράκατε παρὰ τοῦ πατρὸς ποιεῖτε (*do what you have seen from the Father*)

   Alexandrian   𝔓[66] 070

   Western   ℵ* is not really a witness for this option; it much more supports option 4).

(4)   ἑωράκατε παρὰ τῷ πατρὶ ὑμῶν ποιεῖτε (*you are doing what you have seen from your father*)

Western   ℵ* attests this option (though with τοῦ πατρός instead of τῷ πατρί), as does D (though with ταῦτα added before ποιεῖτε).
"Caesarean"   28 700. Here Western.
Byzantine   E F G H N Δ Ψ 0250 157 180 205 579 1006 1010 1071 1243 1292 1342 1424 1505 *Byz Lect*

External evidence. The external evidence presents no clear picture. Alexandrian witnesses can be cited for both the presence and the absence of the pronoun ὑμῶν, with most witnesses of other textual traditions including this pronoun. Both verbs (ἠκούσατε and ἑωράκατε) are found in Alexandrian witnesses. We see here the mixed character of the "Caesarean" witnesses: some have an Alexandrian reading (option 2) and some have a Western reading (option 4). The Western textual tradition (options 3 and 4) has ἑωράκατε and ὑμῶν, and this is apparently the source of this reading in the Byzantine tradition (option 4). The Byzantine text has ἑωράκατε in the overwhelming majority of MSS, but the presence of ἠκούσατε (options 1 and 2) in three witnesses normally regarded as Byzantine illustrates how a reading from a different tradition can survive even in very late MSS.

Internal evidence. Question 1: To whom does πατήρ refer (the difference between options 1 and 2, and between options 3 and 4)? Options 2 and 4 give a definite answer to this question (the word ὑμῶν implying that it is the devil, as stated explicitly in verse 44), and this suggests that ὑμῶν is a secondary and explanatory addition. It is hard to see why ὑμῶν (if original) should have been omitted. Question 2: Is ἠκούσατε (options 1 and 2) or ἑωράκατε (options 3 and 4) is original? Reasons can be given for either possibility. If ἠκούσατε was original, a desire to make the two parts of the verse parallel could explain a change to ἑωράκατε (with ἑώρακα in the first part). If ἑωράκατε was original, a scribe may have felt uncomfortable with the implication that the Jews had seen God, thus explaining a change to ἠκούσατε. Internal criteria suggest that ὑμῶν is a secondary addition, but it is difficult to decide whether ἠκούσατε or ἑωράκατε is the original reading.

Considering all these factors, option 1 is likely, though the {B} rating may seem an overconfident assessment. There are too many uncertainties.

Verse 39

(1)   ἐποιεῖτε (*if you are ... , you would be doing*)
Alexandrian   𝔓75 ℵ* B2 W 070 0141 0250 157 828
Western   D

"Caesarean"   Θ 13 28. More probably Alexandrian than Western.
Byzantine   E F G H 1292 1342 1424 1505 *Byz*[pt] *Lect*[pt,AD]

(2) ἐποιεῖτε ἄν (same meaning but ἄν makes the grammar more "correct")
Alexandrian   ℵ² C L Δ Ψ 33 205 579 892 1071 1243
"Caesarean"   *f*¹ *f*¹³ 565. Here Alexandrian.
Byzantine   N 180 597 1006 1010 *Byz*[pt] *Lect*[pt]

(3) ποιεῖτε (*if you are* ... , *do* [imperative])
Alexandrian   𝔓⁶⁶ B*
"Caesarean"   700 (but with ἄν included). Here Alexandrian.

External evidence. If ἄν is secondary (as suggested below), the only question is whether ἐποιεῖτε (imperfect) or ποιεῖτε (present) is original. Options 1 and 2 both support ἐποιεῖτε, and have the vast majority of evidence from all traditions. Option 3 has the impressive support of 𝔓⁶⁶ B, but these witnesses are overwhelmed by the evidence on the other side.

Internal evidence. It seems probable that ἄν is a secondary addition for the sake of improving or correcting the grammar. The grammatical possibilities and the textual implications may be set out as follows:

(a) Mixed condition. In conditional sentences, different combinations are possible, according to what the writer wishes to say. Option 1 is a mixed condition, with the protasis (the *if* clause) implying something factual (not hypothetical) and the apodosis (the main clause) implying something contrary to fact. The meaning of this reading is something like this: *if you are Abraham's children (which I agree is true), you would be doing Abraham's works (which you are not doing)*. Such a mixed condition is quite possible, though "correct" grammar would normally require ἄν in the apodosis.

(b) Condition contrary to fact. Normally imperfect in the protasis, and imperfect + ἄν in the apodosis. If a scribe thought that this was the intended meaning, it would explain why he would add ἄν if the word was absent from his exemplar. It also explains why we find ἦτε (imperfect) rather than ἐστε (present) in many MSS (as noted in the *Textual Commentary* but not in the UBS⁴ or UBS⁵ apparatus). The meaning of this reading is something like this: *if you were Abraham's children (which you are not), you would be doing Abraham's works (which you are not doing)*.

(c) Condition of fact. This is seen in option 3, where the protasis implies what is true (as in the first possibility), and the apodosis is a challenge (imperative mood) arising from this. The meaning: *if you are Abraham's children (as I agree), then do Abraham's works.*

External evidence points to ἐποιεῖτε (supported by options 1 and 2) as original. Transcriptional probability suggests that ἄν is secondary; if it were original, it is not likely to have been omitted. Option 3 is the easiest reading (with no grammatical problem), and therefore is least likely to be original. All these considerations indicate option 1 as the earliest form.

Verse 57

(1) ἑώρακας (*have you seen Abraham?*)
     Alexandrian   𝔓⁶⁶ א² B² C L Δ Ψ 0141 0233 33 157 205 579 892 1071
                        1241 1243. B* W (ἑώρακες) have essentially the same
                        reading but with an "incorrect" verb ending.
     Western   D
     "Caesarean"   Θ (actually ἑώρακες - see explanation above) ƒ¹ ƒ¹³ 28
                        565 700. Here Alexandrian.
     Byzantine   A E F G H N 180 597 1006 1010 1292 1342 1424 1505
                        Byz Lect

(2) ἑώρακέν σε (*has Abraham seen you?*)
     Alexandrian   𝔓⁷⁵ א* 070

External evidence. Both options have early attestation, though the first is far more strongly represented, not only by the quantity of MSS but by a variety of textual traditions.

Internal evidence. Would John have written of Jesus seeing Abraham or Abraham seeing Jesus? And which is the more likely direction of scribal change? The *Textual Commentary* suggests that a scribe has changed (1) to (2) in the light of verse 56 (*Abraham saw my day*). This is possible, but it is also possible that a scribe changed an original (2) to (1) to give both verbs (ἔχεις and ἑώρακας/-ες) the same 2nd person singular subject.

Internal considerations are not decisive, but the range of external witnesses points to option 1 as original. If the 2nd person verb is regarded as the earlier reading, the form ἑώρακες (attested in at least three important uncials, plus 28 according to the *Textual Commentary*) should be seriously considered, in view of the known confusion between -ας and -ες in Hellenistic Greek 2nd person singular verb endings.

Verse 59

(1) ἱεροῦ (*out of the temple*)
Alexandrian   𝔓⁶⁶ 𝔓⁷⁵ ℵ* B W
Western   D
"Caesarean"   Θ*. Here most probably Alexandrian.

(2) ἱεροῦ καὶ διελθὼν διὰ μέσου αὐτῶν (*out of the temple and having passed through their midst*)
Alexandrian   ℵ²
"Caesarean"   13 (though without καί). Here Alexandrian.
Byzantine   *l*²¹¹ *l*⁸¹³ . Normally considered Byzantine, but here preserving a non-Byzantine, presumably Alexandrian, reading.

(3) ἱεροῦ διελθὼν διὰ μέσου αὐτῶν καὶ παρῆγεν οὕτως (*out of the temple, having passed through their midst, and thus passed by*)
"Caesarean"   Θᶜ *f*¹ *f*¹³ 28 565 700. Without other Alexandrian or Western support for this reading, it is impossible to know if this is an early reading. In these late and mostly Category III MSS it might be purely Byzantine.
Byzantine   A E F G H Δ 0233 157 180 205 1006 1243 1292 1342 1424 1505 *Byz Lect*

(4) ἱεροῦ καὶ διελθὼν διὰ μέσου αὐτῶν ἐπορεύετο καὶ παρῆγεν οὕτως (*out of the temple and having gone through their midst he went and thus passed by*)
Alexandrian   ℵ¹ C L Ψ 070 0141 33 579 892 1071 1241
Byzantine   N 597 1010

External evidence. All four options have some measure of early support, though less so for options 2 and 3. The first has the strongest support from the Alexandrian tradition, as well as from other textual traditions apart from the Byzantine. Option 2 represents a possibly early expansion of the text, which has survived in some Byzantine witnesses (*l*²¹¹ *l*⁸¹³), though it can hardly be described as a Byzantine reading. The Byzantine textual tradition is seen in option 3; its appearance in A indicates that it originated quite early.

Internal evidence. The apparatus reference to Luke 4:30 after option 2, 3 and 4 provides the necessary clue to the longer readings. The implication is that this passage in John has been influenced by the description from a roughly parallel context in Luke. A scribe may have been motivated to emphasise the impression of a miraculous escape. If any of the longer readings was original, there is no obvious reason for a scribe to have abbreviated the passage. Also, the different forms of the longer readings are a sign that they are secondary. Option 1 is the shortest reading and also not influenced by harmonising tendencies.

Overall, option 1 is supported by both external and internal arguments.

oooOOOooo

With these examples as your guide, it would be good to do some practice on other passages. You can choose any portion of the NT. It might be helpful to continue with John's Gospel, using appendix 2 for information on the MSS. Appendix 1 has similar information and is relevant to any part of the NT. Follow the same steps that we have used already:

1   List each variant separately (the Greek words, precisely; then a literal English translation if you are able).
2   List the evidence, especially the Greek witnesses, under the text-type headings (Alexandrian, Western, "Caesarean", Byzantine).
3   Analyse the external evidence.
4   Consider which criteria related to internal evidence are relevant.
5   Offer an opinion as to which reading may be the earliest.

Chapter 15

FURTHER EXAMPLES OF VARIANTS: SYNOPTIC GOSPELS

Previous chapters have given us a good foundation for being able to evaluate the external evidence in any particular case. The comments on the passages under consideration in this chapter and the next will focus on internal criteria. External criteria will be mentioned briefly and in summary form; they will not be analysed in detail, in contrast to chapter 14. This should *not* be interpreted to mean that the external criteria are not important; the present author is of the view that external criteria should be taken into account more than they are. However, we also need to know how the internal criteria can be applied, and these two chapters provide an opportunity to illustrate this.

Matthew 8:10

Option 1   παρ' οὐδενὶ τοσαύτην πίστιν ἐν τῷ Ἰσραὴλ εὗρον (*with no one did I find such faith in Israel*)

Option 2   οὐδὲ ἐν τῷ Ἰσραὴλ τοσαύτην πίστιν εὗρον (*not even in Israel did I find such faith*)

Option 2 is a harmonisation with Luke 7:9, and is a smoother reading (compared to the rather clumsy phrasing of the first with its two prepositional phrases). It is hard to imagine option 2 being changed to option 1. Option 1 has adequate external support, though not large in quantity.

Matthew 11:2

Option 1   διὰ τῶν μαθητῶν (*through the disciples*)
Option 2   δύο τῶν μαθητῶν (*two of the disciples*)
Option 3   *discipulos* (Latin) (*disciples*)

External evidence would suggest that option 1 is the earliest reading. This conclusion is supported by any or all of these internal factors: (a) to "send *through* someone" is an unusual expression, and likely to be corrected to something easier; (b) when we recognise that the vowels ι and υ had a very similar pronunciation (*ee*), we can see how a scribe might have changed διά to δύο; (c) the reading δύο could be the result of harmonisation with Luke 7:18.

Matthew 11:15

Option 1   ὦτα (*he who has ears, let him hear*)
Option 2   ὦτα ἀκούειν (*he who has ears to hear, let him hear* OR *he who has ears, let him certainly hear*)

The exhortation about careful hearing contained in this verse is found in several other Synoptic passages, in both shorter and longer forms. Here UBS mentions 13:9, 43 (where the shorter text is printed but where the longer form is also found as a variant), but other passages can also be cited, such as Mark 4:9 and Luke 8:8 where the longer form is found (without any variant as far as we are informed in UBS and NA).

Intrinsic probability is indecisive, for both the shorter and longer forms of this saying are found in the MSS in all three examples in Matthew. Several arguments from transcriptional probability could apply. As the longer form is apparently more common, it could be argued that the scribal tendency to harmonise caused an earlier shorter text to be expanded. The other possibility is that a scribe was uncomfortable with the un-Greek expression ἀκούειν ἀκουέτω (*let him certainly hear* or *let him make sure he hears*) which could derive from the Hebrew infinitive absolute construction. In that case an earlier longer text would have been abbreviated by omitting the word ἀκούειν.

This is a good example where internal criteria are in conflict. Option 1 is supported by: (a) general preference for the shorter reading; and (b) preference for the non-harmonising reading. But option 2 is supported by: (a) preference for the more Semitic form of expression; and (b) preference for the more difficult reading.

External support for option 1 appears small, but the evidence of B D 700 is significant, covering several text-types.

Matthew 11:19

Option 1   ἀπὸ τῶν ἔργων (*by her deeds*)
Option 2   ἀπὸ πάντων τῶν ἔργων (*by all her deeds*)
Option 3   ἀπὸ τῶν τέκνων (*by her children*)
Option 4   ἀπὸ πάντων τῶν τέκνων (*by all her children*)

The word πάντων is poorly attested and clearly secondary. The same can be said of τέκνων, though it has much better external support. Both πάντων and τέκνων are explained as harmonisation with Luke 7:35. Option 1 has strong external support, even if not large in quantity.

Matthew 12:15

Option 1   ὄχλοι πολλοί (*many crowds*)
Option 2   πολλοί (*many people*)
Option 3   ὄχλοι (*crowds*)

External evidence suggests option 1 or option 2. Option 2 is the shorter reading, and has satisfactory external support. Option 1 may represent harmonisation with other passages in Matthew where ὄχλοι πολλοί occurs (eg 4:25, 8:1); or it may be the result of conflation, if the reading of option 3 existed earlier than its sole extant witness.

Matthew 18:15

Option 1   ἁμαρτήσῃ εἰς σέ (*sins against you*)
Option 2   ἁμάρτῃ εἰς σέ (*sins against you*)
Option 3   ἁμαρτήσῃ (*sins*)
Option 4   ἁμάρτῃ (*sins*)

Did εἰς σέ belong to the original or not? The combined evidence for options 1 and 2 suggests so (despite the witness of א B for option 3), as well as intrinsic probability, since the context describes a private matter between two people. If option 1 (or 2) is original, the omission of εἰς σέ may have been deliberate, in order to generalise the passage and make it relevant to any situation where sin is committed. The second aorist ἁμάρτῃ (instead of first aorist ἁμαρτήσῃ) may have been suggested by Luke 17:3.

Matthew 19:29

Option 1   πατέρα ἢ μητέρα (*father or mother*)
Option 2   πατέρα ἢ μητέρα ἢ γυναῖκα (*father or mother or wife*)
Option 3   μητέρα (*mother*)
Option 4   γονεῖς (*parents*)

If option 1 is original, harmonisation would explain options 2 and 4 (Luke 18:29), and homoeoteleuton (haplography) would explain option 3, where the scribe after writing ἀδελφὰς ἢ looks back to the wrong ἢ and writes μητέρα as the next word (thus omitting πατέρα ἢ). Conversely, if option 2 were the original reading, harmonisation with Mark 10:29 would explain the omission of γυναῖκα. The choice is between options 1 and 2, with external evidence perhaps suggesting option 2, with B providing the only substantial external support for option 1.

Matthew 20:31

Option 1   ἐλέησον ἡμᾶς, κύριε (*have mercy on us, Lord*)
Option 2   ἐλέησον ἡμᾶς (*have mercy on us*)
Option 3   κύριε, ἐλέησον ἡμᾶς (*Lord, have mercy on us*)

In favour of option 3 is its very good external support, and the possibility that option 1 could have arisen by assimilation to verse 30 (most witnesses that support option 1 have the same form of words in verse 30). In favour of option 1, a scribe may have changed produced option 3 in preference for a form of words familiar from the church's liturgy. Option 2 can be explained by assimilation (to 9:27, Mark 10:48, Luke 18:39).

Matthew 22:30

Option 1   ἄγγελοι (*angels*)
Option 2   οἱ ἄγγελοι (*the angels*)
Option 3   ἄγγελοι θεοῦ (*angels of God*)
Option 4   ἄγγελοι τοῦ θεοῦ (*angels of God*)

The words (τοῦ) θεοῦ are a natural complement, more likely to have been added to an original shorter text than omitted from an original longer text.

Matthew 23:4

Option 1   βαρέα καὶ δυσβάστακτα (*heavy and difficult to bear*)
Option 2   βαρέα (*heavy*)
Option 3   μεγάλα βαρέα (*large heavy*)
Option 4   δυσβάστακτα (*difficult to bear*)

There is a conflict between external evidence (clearly supporting option 1) and internal evidence, which favours option 2: this is the shorter reading; it is hard to see why δυσβάστακτα, if original, should have omitted; conflation of options 2 and 4 could explain option 1 (if the reading of option 4 existed earlier than its extant attestation).

Matthew 27:16

Option 1   Ἰησοῦν Βαραββᾶν (*Jesus Barabbas*)
Option 2   Βαραββᾶν (*Barabbas*)

Here is another conflict between external and internal evidence. Option 1 does not have as much external support as option 2. But internal factors point to this as the original reading. It is easy to see why an original

'Ιησοῦν would be omitted (out of reverence for Jesus and in horror that the criminal Barabbas would share the same name), but almost impossible to explain why anyone would think to add 'Ιησοῦν to Βαραββᾶν. External evidence suggests that the omission was made quite early.

Mark 1:41

Option 1   σπλαγχνισθείς (*being compassionate*)
Option 2   ὀργισθείς (*being angry*)
Option 3   *Omit*

It is easy to imagine that a reference to Jesus being angry, if original, might have been changed to something softer. But the originality of σπλαγχνισθείς is not only supported by external evidence but by the observation that scribes did not feel the need to alter other references to Jesus' anger (3:5, 10:14). Option 3 is best explained as harmonisation with the parallel passages (Matthew 8:3, Luke 5:13), and is in any case very poorly attested. The change from σπλαγχνισθείς to ὀργισθείς could be explained as the creative editing of D (or its predecessor), perhaps prompted by the harshness seen in ἐμβριμησάμενος (*speaking harshly*) in verse 43.

Mark 3:16

Option 1   καὶ ἐποίησεν τοὺς δώδεκα καί (*and he appointed the twelve and*)
Option 2   καί (*and*)
Option 3   πρῶτον Σίμωνα καί (*first Simon and*)
Option 4   καὶ περιάγοντας κηρύσσειν τὸ εὐαγγέλιον. καί (*and as they went around to proclaim the gospel. And*)

The first four words of option 1 create what may have been seen as a clumsy and unnecessary repetition (from verse 14), which may explain why they were deliberately omitted in many witnesses (option 2), unless it was an accidental omission due to the repetition of καί, an example of haplography. Options 3 and 4 are poorly attested externally. Option 3 reflects the same omission, though also adding reference to Simon, as a way of introducing the following statement, and option 4 appears to be a creative rewriting found in part of the Western tradition. Clumsy expression in Mark is no great surprise; the author may have felt this necessary in order to pick up the thread from the beginning of verse 14.

Mark 3:32

Option 1   σου καὶ αἱ ἀδελφαί σου (*your brothers and your sisters*)
Option 2   σου (*your brothers*)

Option 2 has better external support, and it may be questioned whether Jesus' sisters would have made such a confrontational public appearance. If this is original, option 1 may have arisen through a scribe feeling that mention of Jesus' spiritual sister in verse 35 needed a reference to his sisters in verse 32. Arguments in support of option 1 are more difficult to find. It has less impressive external support. If original, the shorter text could be explained as an accidental omission, an example of haplography due to the repetition of σου.

Mark 7:4

Option 1   καὶ χαλκίων καὶ κλινῶν (*and bronze vessels and couches*)
Option 2   καὶ χαλκίων (*and bronze vessels*)
Option 3   *Omit*

External and internal evidence conflicts. Stronger (though fewer) witnesses support option 2. But transcriptional probability favours option 1, with option 2 arising as an accidental omission (due to haplography, repetition of καί) or as deliberate omission of a phrase which did not seem to fit very naturally in the list of items. If option 2 was original, it is not easy to find a convincing explanation for adding καὶ κλινῶν.

Mark 8:38

Option 1   τοὺς ἐμοὺς λόγους (*my words*)
Option 2   τοὺς ἐμούς (*my people*)

External evidence strongly favours option 1. The shorter reading (in which τοὺς ἐμούς means *my people* or *my disciples*) could have arisen through homoeoteleuton (the repeated ending -ους).

Mark 9:49

Option 1   πᾶς γὰρ πυρὶ ἁλισθήσεται (*for everyone will be salted with fire*)
Option 2   πᾶς γὰρ πυρὶ ἁλισθήσεται καὶ πᾶσα θυσία ἁλὶ ἁλισθήσεται (*for everyone will be salted with fire and every sacrifice will be salted with salt*)
Option 3   πᾶσα γὰρ θυσία ἁλὶ ἁλισθήσεται (*for every sacrifice will be salted with salt*)
Option 4   *Omnia substantia consumitur* (Latin: *all their substance will be consumed*)

Option 1 has sufficiently strong external support to suggest that it was the original reading. It is a difficult saying and at some stage the words of

Leviticus 2:13 may have been written in the margin as an attempted explanation. The next step was the addition of these words to the text, either alongside the original reading (option 2) or instead of it (option 3). Option 4 (representing the Greek πᾶσα δὲ οὐσία ἀναλωθήσεται) can be explained as a misreading of option 3, with οὐσία (ΟΥΣΙΑ) written by mistake for θυσία (ΘΥΣΙΑ), and ἀναλωθήσεται (ΑΝΑΛΩΘΗΣΕΤΑΙ) written by mistake for ἁλὶ ἁλισθήσεται (ΑΛΙΑΛΙΣΘΗΣΕΤΑΙ).

Mark 13:33

Option 1   ἀγρυπνεῖτε (*watch*)
Option 2   ἀγρυπνεῖτε καὶ προσεύχεσθε (*watch and pray*)
Option 3   καὶ ἀγρυπνεῖτε καὶ προσεύχεσθε (*and watch and pray*)

Perhaps it is easier to account for the addition of καὶ προσεύχεσθε to an original shorter text (possibly in harmony with 14:38), than for the omission of these words if original. Option 1 has slightly more impressive external support.

Mark 15:34

Option 1   ἐγκατέλιπές με (*why have you forsaken me?*)
Option 2   με ἐγκατέλιπες (*why have you forsaken me?*)
Option 3   ὠνείδισάς με (*why have you reproached me?*)

Option 3 apparently represents a change made for theological reasons, a scribe finding the idea of Jesus being abandoned by God too difficult. The source of the verb ὀνειδίζω is most likely Romans 15:3 (quoting Psalm 69:9); or less likely Mark 15:32, where the two criminals are reproaching Jesus (though this would mean equating God's treatment of Jesus with that of the criminals). Though options 1 and 2 can both be explained as harmonisation, in line with Psalm 22:2 LXX (option 1) or Matthew 27:46 (option 2), one of these is the original, with option 1 (supported by ℵ B) having slightly the stronger external support.

Variations on the verb ἐγκατέλιπες in some of the MSS are worth noting: ἐγκατέλειπες, due to itacism (where the spellings ι and ει had the same sound and were therefore easily confused), and ἐγκατέλιπας, confusing the correct second aorist ending -ες and the first aorist ending -ας.

Luke 2:14

Option 1   ἐν ἀνθρώποις εὐδοκίας (*among men of [God's] pleasure*). Latin texts with *hominibus bonae voluntatis* also support this option.

Option 2   ἐν ἀνθρώποις εὐδοκία (*among men goodwill*)
Option 3   καὶ ἐν ἀνθρώποις εὐδοκία (*and among men goodwill*)

Option 3 is only a minor variant on option 2. The difference between the two main options (1 and 2) is a single Greek letter. This could have been accidentally omitted in copying, or may be explained as a deliberate change by a scribe not comfortable with this Semitic use of the genitive εὐδοκίας. Option 1 is clearly supported by the weight of external evidence.

Luke 3:22

Option 1   Σὺ εἶ ὁ υἱός μου ὁ ἀγαπητός, ἐν σοὶ εὐδόκησα (*you are my beloved Son, in you I am well pleased*)
Option 2   Σὺ εἶ ὁ υἱός μου ὁ ἀγαπητός, ἐν ᾧ εὐδόκησα (*you are my beloved Son, in whom I am well pleased*)
Option 3   Οὗτός ἐστιν ὁ υἱός μου ὁ ἀγαπητός, ἐν ᾧ εὐδόκησα (*this is my beloved Son, in whom I am well pleased*)
Option 4   Υἱός μου εἶ σύ, ἐγὼ σήμερον γεγέννηκά σε (*you are my Son, today I have begotten you*)

All the variants can be explained as the result of harmonisation. Option 3 (speaking *about* Jesus rather than *to* him) conforms to Matthew 3:17, as well as to Luke's transfiguration account (Luke 9:35), and option 4 conforms to Psalm 2:7. If option 1 is not original, it too could be explained as a harmonisation with Mark 1:11, but the external evidence suggests that it is original; option 2 is a minor variant (with ᾧ instead of σοί).

Luke 5:17

Option 1   αὐτόν (*so that he healed*)
Option 2   αὐτούς (*so that [he] healed them*)
Option 3   πάντας (*so that [he] healed all*)

External evidence points to option 1 as original. The changes are explained as failure to understand the grammar here, ie that αὐτόν is *subject* of the infinitive. Some scribes assumed that the pronoun is the *object* and changed it to something which made sense to them (αὐτούς or πάντας).

Luke 6:35

Option 1   μηδέν (*expecting nothing in return*)
Option 2   μηδένα (*despairing of no one*)

In option 1 the verb ἀπελπίζω means *expect in return*, in option 2 *despair of*. If option 1 is original (as the external evidence suggests), dittography may explain the addition of alpha in option 2 (ie repeating the letter which occurs at the beginning of the following word), unless it is a deliberate change by a scribe not familiar with the sense *expect in return*.

Luke 6:48

Option 1   διὰ τὸ καλῶς οἰκοδομῆσθαι αὐτήν (*because it had been well built*)
Option 2   τεθεμελίωτο γὰρ ἐπὶ τὴν πέτραν (*for it had been founded on the rock*)
Option 3   *Omit*

External evidence favours option 1. Option 2 is a harmonisation with Matthew 7:25. Option 3 could be explained by 𝔓⁴⁵'s tendency to be concise, or perhaps more probably as a result of haplography, due to the preceding αὐτήν.

Luke 9:35

Option 1   ἐκλελεγμένος (*chosen*)
Option 2   ἀγαπητός (*beloved*)
Option 3   ἀγαπητός, ἐν ᾧ εὐδόκησα (*beloved, in whom I am well pleased*)

Luke almost certainly wrote ἐκλελεγμένος, as the external evidence indicates. Harmonisation explains the other readings: option 2 harmonising with Mark 9:7, and option 3 with Matthew 17:5.

Luke 9:59

Option 1   κύριε (*Lord* or *sir*)
Option 2   *Omit*

Option 2 has limited but significant external support (including B and D), and κύριε might easily have been added (perhaps harmonising with Matthew 8:21). Option 1 must be considered on the basis of the strong external evidence, and it is possible that if κύριε was written in abbreviated form (first and last letters KE), it might have been accidentally omitted.

Luke 13:35

Option 1   ἕως ἥξει ὅτε εἴπητε (*until it will come when you say*)
Option 2   ἕως ἂν ἥξῃ ὅτε εἴπητε (*until it will come when you say*)
Option 3   ἕως ἂν ἥξει ὅτε εἴπητε (*until it will come when you say*)

Option 4   ἕως εἴπητε (*until you say*)
Option 5   ἕως ἂν εἴπητε (*until you say*)
Option 6   ἀπ᾽ ἄρτι ἕως ἂν εἴπητε (*from now until you say*)
Option 7   ἀπ᾽ ἄρτι ἕως ἂν ἥξει ὅτε εἴπητε (*from now until it will come when you say*)

The reading which best explains the others is option 1, which contains two grammatical problems which scribes would have been tempted to correct. (a) Feeling that ἕως + future indicative is unsatisfactory, some have added ἄν, or changed future ἥξει to aorist subjunctive ἥξῃ, or both. (b) Though εἴπητε is universally attested, there is also evidence of discomfort about the subjunctive following ὅτε, which explains options 4, 5 and 6, in which ἥξει ὅτε are omitted, leaving εἴπητε as the verb in the ἕως clause. In a case like this the external evidence is inevitably divided and indecisive. The most likely options are 1 (supported only by D) and 4 (supported by 𝔓⁴⁵ B and a small number of other MSS).

Luke 17:9

Option 1   διαταχθέντα; (... *what was commanded?*)
Option 2   διαταχθέντα; οὐ δοκῶ (... *what was commanded? I don't think so!*)
Option 3   διαταχθέντα αὐτῷ; οὐ δοκῶ (... *what was commanded to him? I don't think so!*)

The words οὐ δοκῶ appear to be a comment at first written in the margin, and later transferred by a careless scribe into the text. Likewise, αὐτῷ appears to be a natural addition to an originally shorter text. The short reading is certainly suggested by the external evidence.

Luke 22:31

Option 1   Σίμων (*Simon*)
Option 2   εἶπεν δὲ ὁ κύριος, Σίμων (*the Lord said, Simon*)

The shorter text seems to be the original, as there is no obvious reason why the words εἶπεν δὲ ὁ κύριος, if original, would have been omitted. The most likely reason for the addition was the need to have a suitable introduction to the reading in a liturgical context. Option 2 has a wide range of external support, but just the same it is almost certainly the later reading; option 1 has more limited but good external support.

<u>Luke 24:53</u>

Option 1   εὐλογοῦντες (*blessing*)
Option 2   αἰνοῦντες (*praising*)
Option 3   αἰνοῦντες καὶ εὐλογοῦντες (*praising and blessing*)

This is a classic example of conflation, with the Byzantine tradition preferring to combine two earlier readings rather than choose one and reject the other. The choice is between the first and second options. On the basis of external evidence there seems no obvious way of deciding whether the first (Alexandrian) or the second (Western) is earlier.

Here are some <u>other challenging synoptic passages</u>. No solutions are suggested, but some questions are given to encourage your reflection.

<u>Matthew 8:28</u>

Option 1   Γαδαρηνῶν (*of the Gadarenes*)
Option 2   Γεργεσηνῶν (*of the Gergesenes*)
Option 3   Γερασηνῶν (*of the Gerasenes*)

Was the place Gadara, Gergesa or Gerasa? Consider also Mark 5:1 and Luke 8:26. If Matthew's original text had a different place name to Mark, what does this imply about Matthew's use of Mark as a source?

<u>Matthew 21:29-31</u>

Option 1   The first son was at first unwilling but later changed his mind.
            The second son agreed with the father's request but did not go.
            The first son did the father's will.
Option 2   The same as option 1, except for τῷ δευτέρῳ (verse 30) instead
            of τῷ ἑτέρῳ.
Option 3   The first son was at first unwilling but later changed his mind
            (εἰς τὸν ἀμπελῶνα are added after ἀπῆλθεν).
            The second son agreed with the father's request but did not go.
            The second son (ὁ ἔσχατος) did the father's will.
Option 4   The first son agreed with the father's request but did not go.
            The second son was at first unwilling but later changed his
            mind.
            The second son (ὁ ὕστερος) did the father's will.
Option 5   The same as option 4, though with differences in wording:
            ὑπάγω instead of ἐγώ, κύριε (verse 29), τῷ ἑτέρῳ instead of τῷ
            δευτέρῳ (verse 30), addition of δέ after ὕστερον (verse 30), ὁ
            ἔσχατος instead of ὁ ὕστερος (verse 31).

How did the first son respond? How did the second son respond? Which son did the father's will? Which option do you think is original? How can you explain the other options? Is option 3 (the reading of D and many other Western witnesses) nonsense, or can you work out the possible logic behind this variant?

Luke 10:1

Option 1   ἑβδομήκοντα δύο (72)
Option 2   ἑβδομήκοντα (70)

Did Jesus send 72 or 70 on the mission? The same issue applies to verse 17.

Luke 11:2

Option 1   ἐλθέτω/ἐλθάτω ἡ βασιλεία σου (*let your kingdom come*)
Option 2   ἐλθέτω τὸ πνεῦμά σου τὸ ἅγιον ἐφ᾽ ἡμᾶς καὶ καθαρισάτω ἡμᾶς (*let your Holy Spirit come on us and cleanse us*)
Option 3   ἐφ᾽ ἡμᾶς ἐλθέτω σου ἡ βασιλεία (*let your kingdom come on us*)
Option 4   ἐλθάτω τὸ ἅγιον πνεῦμά σου, ἐλθάτω ἡ βασιλεία σου (*let your Holy Spirit come, let your kingdom come*)

Was reference to the Holy Spirit (options 2 and 4) a genuine part of Luke's version of the Lord's Prayer? If not, where has this come from?

Luke 23:34

The question relates to the words ὁ δὲ Ἰησοῦς ἔλεγεν, Πάτερ, ἄφες αὐτοῖς, οὐ γὰρ οἴδασιν τί ποιοῦσιν (*Jesus said, Father, forgive them, for they do not know what they are doing*).

Option 1   *Omit*
Option 2   *Include, with minor variations*

Was this part of Luke's Gospel? If not, where did these words come from? They are not found in any other Gospel.

Chapter 16

FURTHER EXAMPLES OF VARIANTS:
PAUL'S LONGER LETTERS

This chapter continues in the same pattern as the previous one, with examples from Romans, 1 Corinthians and 2 Corinthians.

Romans 1:31

Option 1   ἀστόργους (*heartless*)
Option 2   ἀστόργους ἀσπόνδους (*heartless, irreconcilable*)

Though it could be argued that ἀσπόνδους accidentally dropped out because of homoeoteleuton (the same ending -ους), the external evidence strongly supports the shorter reading. Another explanation is that option 2 is an example of harmonisation, with ἀσπόνδους added by a scribe familiar with a similar list in 2 Timothy 3:3, where ἄστοργοι is followed by ἄσπονδοι. However, this seems a rather remote parallel.

Romans 4:19

Option 1   κατενόησεν (*he considered*)
Option 2   οὐ κατενόησεν (*he did not consider*)

The options at first sight seem to contradict each other, but they both make good sense, requiring only a different translation of the participle ὑπάρχων. (1): He considered his body dead *because* he was 100 years old. (2): He did not consider his body dead *though* he was 100 years old. If option 1, which has better external support, was original, the addition of οὐ was likely intended to make Abraham's faith seem stronger: he ignored the impotence of his 100 year old body. But option 1 already testifies to his great faith, which stayed strong even when he reflected on the reality of his age.

Romans 5:1

Option 1   ἔχομεν (*we have*)
Option 2   ἔχωμεν (*let us have*)

Is this a statement (indicative ἔχομεν) or an exhortation (subjunctive ἔχωμεν)? External evidence strongly supports the subjunctive, though the apparent reading of 0220 (late 3rd century) provides early evidence for the indicative. Intrinsic probability suggests the indicative, it being more likely that Paul is here stating the automatic result of God's justifying work, than that he is exhorting his readers to experience peace.

The difference in Greek is a single letter, omicron or omega, which had the same pronunciation in Hellenistic Greek (as still today). This would have made it very easy for a change in either direction to have happened. Indeed, it has even been suggested (*Textual Commentary*) that it was Paul's amanuensis Tertius who wrote ἔχωμεν even though Paul dictated ἔχομεν.

Romans 6:12

Option 1   ταῖς ἐπιθυμίαις αὐτοῦ (*its desires* = the desires of the body)
Option 2   αὐτῇ (*it* = sin)
Option 3   αὐτῇ ἐν ταῖς ἐπιθυμίαις αὐτοῦ (*it in its desires*)

Options 1 and 2 are both early, though it is perhaps easier to see why an original ταῖς ἐπιθυμίαις αὐτοῦ might be replaced by αὐτῇ (in the light of the frequent mention of ἁμαρτία throughout this section) than the opposite. Option 3 is an attempted conflation, requiring also the addition of ἐν.

Romans 8:2

Option 1   σε (*you*)
Option 2   με (*me*)
Option 3   ἡμᾶς (*us*)

Option 3 is externally poorly supported; it seems to derive from option 2 as an attempt to make the passage apply to all believers. Regarding options 1 and 2, on transcriptional grounds σε is more likely: a scribe is much more likely to have changed σε to με than the opposite. On intrinsic grounds, σε appears more difficult: why would Paul have suddenly used a 2nd person singular pronoun? But it is not impossible, for Paul may well have wanted to make the application clear to the individual reader. On the other hand, it is easier to see why a scribe may have changed an original σε to με, to continue the use of the 1st singular pronoun from the preceding section. Arguments from internal evidence are inconclusive, but external evidence favours option 1.

Romans 8:28

Option 1   συνεργεῖ (*he works together* or *all things work together*)
Option 2   συνεργεῖ ὁ θεός (*God works together*)

Option 2 certainly has impressive early external support (though strangely not much subsequently). But it is difficult to see why ὁ θεός, if original, would have been omitted (it can hardly have been accidental), and easy to see why it would have been added, in order to make clear that *God* is the subject of συνεργεῖ and πάντα the object; without ὁ θεός it is possible to take πάντα as the subject, which would make it possible to interpret the statement to mean that all things work out in an impersonal way.

Romans 9:32

Option 1   ἔργων (*works*)
Option 2   ἔργων νόμου (*works of law*)

The longer reading seems to have arisen to conform to Paul's usage in other places (eg 3:20, 28, and often in Galatians). However, Paul is just as likely to have written ἔργων (without νόμου), as in 4:6, 11:6, and the shorter reading has stronger external attestation.

Romans 11:31

Option 1   νῦν (*now*)
Option 2   ὕστερον (*later*)
Option 3   *Omit*

External evidence is ambiguous; for example, all three options have Alexandrian support (option 1 in ℵ B, option 2 in 33, option 3 in 𝔓⁴⁶ A). The reading νῦν produces a difficult sense, as we might think it is surely not *now* but *later* that the Jews will receive mercy. That would explain the introduction of ὕστερον into the text (the easiest reading, but with poorer external support and so evidently secondary). The choice between option 1 (the more difficult) and option 3 (the shorter) is not easy, though it is more likely that an original νῦν was later omitted because of its perceived difficulty than that νῦν was later added. Option 1 is difficult but not impossible, with the sense *so that they too may now be in a position to receive mercy.*

Romans 13:9

Option 1   οὐ κλέψεις, οὐκ ἐπιθυμήσεις (*you will not steal, you will not covet*)
Option 2   οὐ κλέψεις (*you will not steal*)
Option 3   οὐ κλέψεις, οὐ ψευδομαρτυρήσεις, οὐκ ἐπιθυμήσεις (*you will not steal, you will not bear false witness, you will not covet*)
Option 4   οὐ κλέψεις, οὐ ψευδομαρτυρήσεις (*you will not steal, you will not bear false witness*)

Option 5   *Omit*

Which of the ten commandments did Paul include here? It is more likely
that the commandment about false witness (options 3 and 4) is a secondary addition, in harmony with Exodus 20:15-17 and Deuteronomy 5:19-21.
On the other hand, accidental omission of that commandment could be
explained by homoeoteleuton (the verb ending -εις in each case). External
evidence limits the choices to option 1 and option 3, with a strong
inclination to option 1.

Romans 13:11

Option 1   ὑμᾶς (*you*)
Option 2   ἡμᾶς (*us*)

With the pronouns ἡμᾶς and ὑμᾶς there is always the possibility of
accidental change because of the identical (or near identical) sound of η
and υ in Hellenistic Greek. If the change was deliberate, it is more likely
explained as an original ὑμᾶς being changed to ἡμᾶς, either to make the
passage apply to all believers or to conform with the use of the 1st person
plural in the second part of the verse. External evidence is divided.

Romans 14:19

Option 1   διώκωμεν (*let us pursue*)
Option 2   διώκομεν (*we are pursuing*)
Option 3   διώκετε (*pursue*, imperative)

Option 2 is strongly supported by ℵ A B. Confusion of ο and ω in Hellenistic Greek could have led to accidental change from διώκομεν to διώκωμεν
or vice versa. The context is a call to proper Christian behaviour, which
makes an exhortation (subjunctive) more likely on the grounds of intrinsic
probability. This is also the perspective of the lectionaries which have used
the imperative διώκετε, a clearly secondary reading. Thus there is a clash
here between external evidence (option 2) and internal evidence (option 1).

Romans 15:31

Option 1   διακονία (*ministry*)
Option 2   δωροφορία (*gift-bringing*)

Despite its use in B D, δωροφορία seems to be secondary. It has the appearance of a marginal note, an explanation of the nature of Paul's διακονία to
Jerusalem, and at an early stage in the transmission of the text replacing

the original word διακονία in some MSS. We note too that δωροφορία is a very rare word, occurring only twice in later Greek authors and nowhere else in the NT.

1 Corinthians 2:4

Option 1	πειθοῖς σοφίας λόγοις (*persuasive words of wisdom*)
Option 2	πειθοῖς σοφίας (*persuasive things of wisdom*)
Option 3	πειθοῖς ἀνθρωπίνης σοφίας λόγοις (*persuasive words of human wisdom*)
Option 4	πειθοῖ ἀνθρωπίνης σοφίας λόγοις (*persuasion, words of human wisdom*)
Option 5	πειθοῖ σοφίας λόγων (*persuasion of words of wisdom*)

There is little doubt that ἀνθρωπίνης is a secondary addition, but the choice between πειθοῖς (masc dat pl of the adjective πειθός) and πειθοῖ (dat sg of the noun πειθώ) is much more difficult. πειθός occurs nowhere else in Greek literature, and πειθώ is an uncommon type of 3rd declension noun. Whatever the original word happened to be, a scribe might have been tempted to make a change. The difference is only the single letter sigma, which also occurs at the beginning of the next word (σοφίας), and so an accidental change in either direction is also possible (haplography or dittography). External evidence points to πειθοῖς as the likely original.

1 Corinthians 3:3

Option 1	ἔρις (*strife*)
Option 2	ἔρις καὶ διχοστασίαι (*strife and dissensions*)

Galatians 5:20 includes διχοστασίαι in a list of vices several words after ἔρις, and this provides a possible (though not very convincing) explanation for the later addition of the word in the present passage, though if it was a secondary addition, its presence in 𝔓⁴⁶ shows that the change was made quite early. Whatever the reason for the change, it certainly seems that the longer reading is secondary, as there is no clear reason why διχοστασίαι, if original, would have been omitted.

1 Corinthians 3:5

Option 1	Ἀπολλῶς ... Παῦλος (*Apollos ... Paul*)
Option 2	Παῦλος ... Ἀπολλῶς (*Paul ... Apollos*)

There is little doubt that option 1 was original, with option 2 motivated by the desire to give Paul his proper position of honour (as it was thought) at the beginning of the series of questions. There is no obvious reason why option 2, if original, would have been changed to option 1. This conclusion is supported by the external evidence.

1 Corinthians 5:5

Option 1   κυρίου (*the Lord*)
Option 2   κυρίου Ἰησοῦ (*the Lord Jesus*)
Option 3   κυρίου Ἰησοῦ Χριστοῦ (*the Lord Jesus Christ*)
Option 4   κυρίου ἡμῶν Ἰησοῦ Χριστοῦ (*our Lord Jesus Christ*)

The four options demonstrate the tendency to add appropriate honorific titles in references to Jesus. Option 1, the shortest and least embellished, is the original, with limited though adequate MS attestation as well as support from early patristic sources.

1 Corinthians 6:14

Option 1   ἐξεγερεῖ (*will raise*)
Option 2   ἐξήγειρεν (*raised*)
Option 3   ἐξεγείρει (*raises*)

Is the resurrection of the believer described here as future (option 1), past (option 2) or present (option 3)? All three can be defended exegetically, and all three have credible external support. $\mathfrak{P}^{46}$ offers an insight into what might have happened. The original scribe of $\mathfrak{P}^{46}$ wrote ἐξεγείρει, then corrected it himself to ἐξεγερεῖ (either from his own view that the future was more appropriate or because he noticed that he had made a mistake when copying from his exemplar). A later corrector of $\mathfrak{P}^{46}$ wrote ἐξήγειρεν, perhaps to conform to ἤγειρεν in the first part of the verse. External evidence is certainly divided, but option 1 (future) seems most likely on intrinsic grounds, as a parallel to καταργήσει in verse 13.

1 Corinthians 10:2

Option 1   ἐβαπτίσθησαν (*they were baptised*)
Option 2   ἐβαπτίσαντο (*they got themselves baptised*)
Option 3   ἐβαπτίζοντο (*they were getting themselves baptised*)

Was an original middle (ἐβαπτίσαντο) changed to a passive (ἐβαπτίσθησαν) by a scribe influenced by the practice of Christian baptism in which a convert was baptised by someone else, or an original passive to the middle by a scribe aware of Jewish practice where a person baptised him/herself or got him/herself baptised? The imperfect tense of option 3 (only in 𝔓⁴⁶*) could be either middle or passive. External evidence is divided.

1 Corinthians 11:29

Option 1   σῶμα (*body*)
Option 2   σῶμα τοῦ κυρίου (*body of the Lord*)
Option 3   αἷμα τοῦ κυρίου (*blood of the Lord*)

Option 2 expands option 1 by seeking to specify the meaning of σῶμα, ie it is the body of *Christ* offered in sacrifice that the person fails to discern, rather than the body of *Christ's people*, the church. If τοῦ κυρίου belonged to the original text, it is difficult to see why it would have been omitted. Indeed, it is possible that Paul was deliberately ambiguous here, allowing for both applications of the word σῶμα. The introduction of the word αἷμα in option 3 seems to be an attempt to make the noun more suitable to the closest verb πίνει. Option 1 certainly has the strongest external support.

1 Corinthians 13:3

Option 1   καυχήσωμαι (*that I may boast*)
Option 2   καυθήσομαι (*that I may be burned*)
Option 3   καυθήσωμαι (*that I may be burned*)
Option 4   καυθῇ (*that it may be burned*)

Did Paul contemplate giving up his body as a ground of boasting (option 1) or in order to be burned (options 2, 3 and 4)? The concept of Paul finding reason for boasting is found elsewhere, and so the reading καυχήσωμαι is intrinsically possible. On the other hand, by the time our extant MSS were produced many Christians had suffered martyrdom by fire, and so it is not hard to see why *boast* (καυχάομαι) may have been replaced by *burn* (καίω), especially as the change involved only one letter (in the case of καυθήσωμαι) or two (in the case of καυθήσομαι). It is harder to find reasons for changing *burn* to *boast*.

καυθήσομαι would be an unusual example of a future indicative in a ἵνα clause, with καυθήσωμαι an alternative spelling (ο and ω having the same pronunciation), just as καυχήσωμαι in 048 is an alternative for καυχήσωμαι. Option 4 may be a grammatical improvement, using a subjunctive form.

Despite the fact that the combined witness for options 2 and 3 (representing essentially the one reading) is significant, the external evidence still favours option 1, and the internal evidence does likewise.

1 Corinthians 15:47

Option 1   ὁ δεύτερος ἄνθρωπος (*the second man*)
Option 2   ὁ δεύτερος ὁ κύριος (*the second, the Lord*)
Option 3   ὁ δεύτερος ἄνθρωπος ὁ κύριος (*the second man, the Lord*)
Option 4   ὁ δεύτερος ἄνθρωπος πνευματικός (*the second man, spiritual*)

External evidence supports option 1 (ὁ δεύτερος ἄνθρωπος), with the others being apparent attempts to clarify the meaning of the phrase, specifically who was the second man and what was his nature. Option 2 reads ὁ δεύτερος ὁ κύριος (*the second [man], the Lord*), option 3 similarly ὁ δεύτερος ἄνθρωπος ὁ κύριος (*the second man, the Lord*). Other options offer further explanations, with 𝔓⁴⁶ reading ἄνθρωπος πνευματικός (*spiritual man*) (option 4), and two Western MSS (F G) adding the words ὁ οὐράνιος (*the heavenly [one]*) at the end of the verse (this variant is not included in the UBS apparatus but can be found in NA).

2 Corinthians 1:12

Option 1   ἁπλότητι (*simplicity*)
Option 2   ἁγιότητι (*holiness*)

The two words could have easily been confused by scribes, because of the similarity in appearance of the second and third letters (ΠΛ and ΓΙ). Option 1 can be supported on intrinsic grounds, with ἁπλότητι considered more appropriate in the context than ἁγιότητι, and the noun ἁγιότης not used elsewhere by Paul. But option 2 (ἁγιότης) can hardly be regarded as out of place in the context, and is supported by stronger external evidence.

2 Corinthians 2:9

Option 1   εἰ (*if*)
Option 2   ᾗ (*by which*)
Option 3   *Omit*

Option 1 has the best external support. The change to ᾗ may have been an accidental confusion between the sounds of ει and η, and the omission (option 3) is explained by homoeoarcton (εἰ εἰς).

2 Corinthians 5:3

Option 1   ἐκδυσάμενοι (*having unclothed ourselves*)
Option 2   ἐκλυσάμενοι (*having grown weary*)
Option 3   ἐνδυσάμενοι (*having clothed ourselves*)

Option 1 is preferred by UBS on the ground that ἐνδυσάμενοι (option 3) is tautologous in company with the words οὐ γυμνοὶ εὑρεθησόμεθα. However, ἐνδυσάμενοι can be seen not as tautologous but as providing the precondition for not being found naked. In that case ἐκδυσάμενοι could be the secondary reading, introduced in order to avoid the *appearance* of tautology. Option 3 has by far the best external attestation. Option 2 is derived from option 1 by mistakenly reading delta Δ as lambda Λ.

2 Corinthians 8:7

Option 1 ἡμῶν ἐν ὑμῖν (*love from us among you*)
Option 2 ὑμῶν ἐν ἡμῖν (*love from you among us*)
Option 3 ὑμῶν ἐν ὑμῖν (*love from you among you*)
Option 4 ἡμῶν ἐν ἡμῖν (*love from us among us*)

Option 2 seems to give the easiest sense (meaning *your love to us*), whereas option 1 (*our love for you*) suggests what may appear to be the strange idea of the Corinthians abounding in Paul's love for them. But option 1 possibly represents a *deliberately* paradoxical item at the end of the list: they do in fact abound in the great love which Paul and his colleagues have shown to them. In that case option 2 is secondary, an attempt to provide a more obvious sense. It is hard to see why an original option 2 would have been changed to option 1, a more difficult reading. Options 1 and 2 both have good external support, but internal considerations favour option 1. Options 3 and 4 make little sense, and appear to be the work of scribes who are either confused or simply careless. The similar sounds of η and υ makes it easy to see how careless mistakes might have been made here.

2 Corinthians 11:3

Option 1 ἀπὸ τῆς ἁπλότητος καὶ τῆς ἁγνότητος (*away from the sincerity and the purity*)
Option 2 ἀπὸ τῆς ἁγνότητος καὶ τῆς ἁπλότητος (*away from the purity and the sincerity*)
Option 3 ἀπὸ τῆς ἁπλότητος (*away from the sincerity*)
Option 4 ἀπὸ τῆς ἁγνότητος (*away from the purity*)

The difference between the two nouns is only ΠΛ in the first and ΓΝ in the second, letters which might easily have been confused. This could explain option 2, where a scribe might have accidentally written the second word first and then, immediately noticing his mistake, rather than try to correct the word he had written, simply added the noun which should have come first. Option 3 and 4 are both explained by haplography: in option 3 the scribe writes ἁπλότητος, but looks back and sees ἁγνότητος in his exemplar and imagines it is the word he has written; in option 4 the scribe's eye skips from the first τῆς to the second. UBS considers option 3 a possibility (as explained in the *Textual Commentary*), with καὶ τῆς ἁγνότητος a possible deliberate addition in the interests of clarifying the sense of ἁπλότητος. Conflation might seem to be possible, but option 1 is earlier than options 3 and 4 and cannot be a conflation of them. External evidence is decisive in this case, strongly favouring option 1.

<u>2 Corinthians 12:1</u>

Option 1   καυχᾶσθαι δεῖ (*it is necessary to boast*)
Option 2   καυχᾶσθαι δή (*indeed to boast*)
Option 3   καυχᾶσθαι δέ (*but to boast*)
Option 4   εἰ καυχᾶσθαι δεῖ (*if it is necessary to boast*)

Options 2, 3 and 4 can all be seen as softening the specific statement of option 1. Option 1 directly states Paul's intention to boast, but the others present the matter as a possibility, and scribes would easily have been tempted to introduce one or other of these alternatives. Option 4 may have been suggested to a scribe by 11:30, a few verses previously, which begins in an identical manner. Option 2 could have arisen accidentally, through the similarity of sound between δεῖ and δή, and option 3 likewise, through omission of a single simple letter. The external evidence favours option 1, though option 3 has significant though limited support.

oooOOOooo

These last two chapters have mainly focussed on the use of internal criteria. We have seen how slippery they can be to handle. Different criteria often suggest different solutions, and the subjective opinion of a scholar decides which criterion is to be preferred. This is not an impossible situation, but it does suggest the need to depend more on external evidence and to return to a more objectively based genealogical method (see pages 31-32 above).

Chapter 17

PASSAGES FOR FURTHER STUDY

The following sections of this chapter list other interesting passages in different categories. Study of several passages from each category will give you a further idea of some of the issues involved in textual criticism and some of the principles used by professional textual critics as they do their work.

(a)   Longer passages omitted from UBS/NA (or considered to be of doubtful authenticity). These are found in some English translations (especially KJV and NKJV). Details for each one may be found in the UBS apparatus. Matthew 17:21, 18:11, 23:14, 27:35b, 28:9a, Mark 7:16, 9:44, 46, 11:26, 15:28, 16:9-20, Luke 9:55b-56a, 17:36, 22:43-44, 23:17, 34a, John 5:3b-4, Acts 8:37, 15:34, 24:6b-8a, 28:29, Romans 8:1b, 11:6b, 16:24, 1 Corinthians 6:20b, Hebrews 2:7b, 1 Peter 4:14b, 1 John 5:7-8.

(b)   Floating passages, which some MSS include at other places (though some omit completely). Matthew 20:28, Luke 22:43-44, 23:17, John 7:53 - 8:11, Romans 16:25-27, 1 Corinthians 14:34-35.

(c)   Passages where there is significant tension between strong external evidence and the claims of the internal evidence. Matthew 1:7-8, 8:18, 21, 11:2, 13:35, 20:23, 22:35, 27:49, 28:15, Mark 6:23, 51, 12:26, 15:12, 39, Luke 7:11, 8:43, 11:14, 33, 17:24, 18:24, 20:27, John 2:15, 5:44, 6:14, 10:8, 18, 12:9, Acts 13:33, Romans 4:19, 11:31, 13:11, 14:19, 1 Corinthians 1:8, 14, 2:10, 2 Corinthians 1:12, 5:3, Galatians 1:6, 2:12, 20, 3:21, Ephesians 6:12, Colossians 1:22, 2:7, 1 Thessalonians 2:7, 2 Thessalonians 2:3, 2 Timothy 1:11, Hebrews 2:8, 12:3, 1 Peter 3:16, Revelation 15:6.

(d)   Passages where a reading may be preferred despite weak or relatively weak external evidence. John 18:1, Acts 4:37, Romans 5:1, 1 Corinthians 10:2, Colossians 1:3, 2 Peter 1:17, Revelation 18:3.

(e)   Passages where there may be deliberate scribal change for reasons of theology or related factors (including ecclesiastical order or custom). Matthew 1:16, 20:31, 24:36, 27:16-17, Mark 6:3, 9:29, 10:19, 15:34, Luke 1:3, 2:33, 5:39, 8:3, 11:4, 42, 12:14, 16:12, 22:43-44, 23:43, 24:42, John 1:13, 3:13, 5:32, 7:8, 39, 11:33, 12:32, 16:13, Acts 1:23, 11:2,

15:32, 33, 18:26, 20:28, Romans 9:4, 1 Corinthians 3:5, 7:3, 8:6, Galatians 2:9, Philippians 1:1, 14, 3:12, Colossians 3:16, 1 Thessalonians 1:5, 2 Timothy 3:14, 1 Peter 2:5, 5:2, 1 John 4:3.

(f)   Passages where the Textus Receptus and the Majority Text differ from one another. This information is based on the textual notes in NKJV. The relevant Greek readings can usually be obtained from NA²⁸. In some cases there is more than one variant in the passage mentioned. Matthew 3:11, 4:10, 5:27, 47, 6:18, 7:14, 8:15, 9:36, 10:8, 25, 12:8, 24, 35, 13:15, 18:19, 29, 21:1, 23:21, 25, 25:44, 26:26, 52, 27:35, 41, 42, 28:19, Mark 3:32, 4:4, 9, 6:15, 33, 44, 8:14, 9:40, 11:1, 4, 13:9, 15:32, 16:8, Luke 3:2, 4:8, 6:9, 10, 26, 7:31, 8:3, 9:23, 10:12, 20, 22, 11:15, 13:15, 35, 14:5, 15, 17:4, 9, 36, 19:29, 20:5, 19, 31, 22:60, 23:25, John 1:28, 2:17, 22, 6:45, 7:16, 29, 33, 8:2, 4, 5, 6, 7, 9, 10, 11, 54, 10:8, 13:25, 16:3, 15, 33, 17:2, 11, 20, 18:15, 19:28, 20:29, Acts 3:20, 24, 5:23, 25, 41, 7:37, 8:37, 9:5, 17, 10:6, 21, 39, 12:25, 13:17, 23, 15:11, 22, 34, 17:18, 19:16, 20:8, 28, 34, 21:29, 24:9, 20, 26:17, 27:17, Romans 15:7, 14, 16:18, 25-27, 1 Corinthians 7:34, 11:15, 27, 12:2, 15:39, 49, 2 Corinthians 1:11, 2:17, 8:4, 24, Galatians 4:24, Ephesians 1:10, 18, 3:9, 4:6, Philippians 1:23, 3:3, 4:3, Colossians 1:6, 14, 27, 2:20, 1 Thessalonians 2:2, 11, 2 Thessalonians 1:10, 3:6, 1 Timothy 5:4, 6:5, 2 Timothy 1:1, 2:19, Titus 2:8, Philemon 6, 7, Hebrews 2:7, 4:2, 6:3, 18, 10:9, 11:13, 26, 12:7, 20, 28, 13:9, 21, James 4:2, 12, 13, 5:9, 12, 1 Peter 1:8, 12, 2:21, 3:18, 20, 5:8, 10, 2 Peter 2:3, 3:2, 1 John 1:4, 3:1, 23, 5:4, 7-8, 2 John 3, 3 John 11, Jude 12, 24, Revelation 1:5, 6, 8, 9, 11, 17, 19, 20, 2:15, 19, 20, 21, 22, 24, 3:2, 4, 8, 11, 14, 16, 4:3, 4, 5, 6, 8, 11, 5:4, 5, 6, 10, 13, 14, 6:1, 3, 12, 15, 7:5, 14, 17, 8:7, 13, 9:19, 21, 10:4, 5, 11, 11:1, 4, 8, 9, 12, 15, 17, 19, 12:8, 17, 13:1, 5, 7, 14, 17, 14:1, 4, 5, 8, 12, 13, 15, 15:2, 3, 5, 16:1, 5, 6, 7, 14, 16, 17:1, 4, 8, 16, 18:2, 5, 6, 8, 14, 20, 19:1, 5, 6, 12, 14, 15, 17, 18, 20:4, 10, 12, 14, 21:2, 5, 6, 7, 8, 9, 10, 14, 23, 24, 26, 27, 22:1, 6, 8, 9, 11, 13, 15, 18, 19, 21.

(g)   Passages where the *Textual Commentary²* records the view of dissenting members of the committee, contrary to the majority decision. Matthew 23:4, Mark 3:32, 10:2, Luke 10:1, John 1:3-4, 18, 14:7, Acts 2:38, 10:17, 16:12, 25:17, 26:4, Romans 15:33, 1 Corinthians 10:2, 2 Corinthians 1:10, 4:6, 14, 5:3, Galatians 1:15, Colossians 1:22, 1 Thessalonians 2:7, Hebrews 12:3, James 5:4, 20, 1 Peter 1:12, 5:10, 2 Peter 2:11, Jude 5, Revelation 19:11.

(h)   Passages suspected by Westcott & Hort of containing a primitive error, where the original reading is not contained in any extant witness and where conjectural emendation is required. Matthew 21:28 ff, 28:7, Mark 4:28, Luke 11:35, John 4:1, 6:4, 8:9, Acts 4:25, 7:46,

12:25, 13:32, 43, 16:12, 19:40, 20:28, 25:13, Romans 1:32, 4:12, 5:6, 7:2, 13:3, 15:32, 1 Corinthians 12:2, 2 Corinthians 3:3, 17, 7:8, 12:7, Galatians 5:1, Colossians 2:2, 18, 23, 2 Thessalonians 1:10, 1 Timothy 4:3, 6:7, 2 Timothy 1:13, Philemon 9, Hebrews 4:2, 10:1, 11:4, 37, 12:11, 13:21, 1 Peter 1:7, 3:21, 2 Peter 3:10, 12, 1 John 5:10, Jude 1, 5, 22-23, Revelation 1:20, 2:12, 13, 3:1, 7, 14, 9:10, 11:3, 13:10, 15, 16, 18:12, 19:13.

(i) Passages rated {D} in UBS[3]. Matthew 5:11, 6:15, 8:18, 11:23, 14:24, 27, 15:6, 38, 16:2-3, 12, 20:30, 23:26, 27:5, Mark 1:40, 41, 3:7-8, 5:21 (two passages), 42, 6:20, 22, 23, 7:9, 10:7, 12:23, 14:68, 15:12, Luke 2:15, 8:26, 37, 43, 10:15, 11:13, 14, 33, 12:20, 27, 13:35, 17:23, 18:11, 24, 21:19, 24:3, 6, 9, 12, 36, 40, 47, 51, 52, John 1:21, 5:2, 7:10, 12, 8:44, 9:4 (two passages), 10:29, 12:32, 13:18, 14:17, 15:8, 21:23, Acts 2:16, 44, 3:6, 4:25, 7:16, 10:30, 12:25, 13:18, 20, 33 (two passages), 16:12, 13, 17:3, 26, 18:7, 19:40, 21:23, 24:6-8, 27:27, 28:13, Romans 3:25, 5:6, 8:2, 11, 11:31, 14:19, 1 Corinthians 1:14, 2:4, 15, 5:4, 7:13, 34, 14:39, 2 Corinthians 1:10, 12, 5:3, 7:8, 8:7, 19, 12:7, Galatians 1:6, 8, 15, 4:25, 5:21, Ephesians 3:9, 4:28, 6:12, Philippians 1:14, Colossians 1:3, 20, 22, 2:23, 3:6, Hebrews 3:2, 11:11, 37, 12:3, 13:15, James 3:3, 4:14, 5:20, 1 Peter 3:18, 5:8, 2 Peter 1:3, 2:4, 6, 11, 3:10, 18, 1 John 2:20, 3:13, 19, Jude 5, Revelation 1:15, 13:15, 19:7, 21:3 (two passages).

(j) Passages rated {D} in UBS[4]. Matthew 23:26, Mark 7:9, John 10:29, Acts 16:12, Romans 14:19, 1 Corinthians 7:34, 2 Peter 3:10, Jude 5, Revelation 18:3.

(k) Passages rated {D} in UBS[5]. Matthew 23:26, Mark 7:9, John 10:29, Acts 16:12, Romans 14:19, 1 Corinthians 7:34, Revelation 18:3. These are the same as in UBS[4], except the passages which fall within the *ECM* (2 Peter 3:10, Jude 5) which are now rated {C}. On the other hand there are 42 passages in the catholic epistles marked with a diamond which are now effectively rated {D} in UBS[5] (see chapter 11 above).

(l) Passages upgraded to an {A} rating in UBS[4]. These passages are rated {B} in UBS[3] unless otherwise indicated. This list does not include {A} rated passages which do not appear at all in the apparatus of UBS[3]. Matthew 1:11, 16, 4:10, 17, 7:14, 9:8, 14:3, 17:20, 21, 18:26, 19:16, 17, 21:39, 23:13, 27:4, 28:9, 20, Mark 3:8, 7:16, 8:38, 10:19 {C}, 10:40, 14:5, 24, Luke 1:28, 35, 46, 66, 2:14, 38, 5:17, 39, 39, 6:4 {C}, 10 {C}, 48, 7:10 {C}, 39 {C}, 9:26, 55-56 {C}, 10:22, 11:2, 12:21, 15:21, 16:12, 17:36, 19:25 {C}, 22:43-44 {C}, 62 {C}, 23:15 {C}, 17, 34 {C}, 38, 24:53, John 4:9 {C}, 5:32, 6:1, 15, 27, 7:1, 8:16 {C}, 34 {C}, 11:25,

12:1, 8 {C}, 28, 13:37 {C}, 14:14, Acts 1:11 {C}, 2:18 {C}, 18, 19, 24, 37, 44 {D}, 4:6 {C}, 5:37, 8:10, 9:31, 15:20, 24, 29, 29, 34, 16:36, 17:4, 27 {C}, 28 {C}, 18:21, 25, 20:28, 21:1 {C}, 22:26, 26:28, 27:5, 39, 28:1, 16, 29, Romans 1:7, 15, 5:1 {C}, 6:11, 8:21 {C}, 26, 35, 9:23, 33, 10:17, 11:1, 32, 13:1 {C}, 14:9, 15:7, 29, 31, 33, 16:20, 24, 27 {C}, 1 Corinthians 1:4, 13, 7:14, 8:3 (part {B} & part {C}), 7, 11:24, 29 {C}, 12:9, 2 Corinthians 1:6-7, 2:9, 3:2 {C}, 5:17, 12:1, 13:4, Galatians 2:1, 5, 12, 20, 4:6, 7, 14, 26, Ephesians 3:19, 4:9, 5:2, 9, 30, 6:19, Philippians 1:11, 2:12, 3:16, 4:3, 23, Colossians 1:2, 3:16, 16, 1 Thessalonians 1:1, 5:27, 28, 2 Thessalonians 2:4, 3:16, 18 {C}, 1 Timothy 2:7, 3:1, 16, 6:7 {C}, 19, 21 {C}, 2 Timothy 4:10, 22, Titus 1:4, 3:15, Philemon 25, Hebrews 2:9, 3:6, 4:3, 6:2, 3, 8:11, 9:10, 10:11, 34, 12:1, 13:21, 25 {C}, James 1:3, 12, 5:4 {C}, 1 Peter 1:7, 8, 22 {C}, 2:21, 21, 3:15, 16, 21 {C}, 4:1, 14, 5:14 {C}, 14 {C}, 2 Peter 1:10, 21, 2:15, 18 {C}, 3:9, 1 John 1:4, 2:25, 3:1, 5 {C}, 14 {C}, 4:3 {C}, 3, 19, 20, 5:6, 10, 20, 2 John 3, 8 {C}, 9, 13, 3 John 4, Jude 1, 3, Revelation 1:5, 8, 2:22, 5:9 {C}, 10 {C}, 6:17 {C}, 10:6, 11:2, 13:7, 17 {C}, 18, 14:13, 20:9 {C}, 22:14, 21.

PART III

FOR REFLECTION

Chapter 18

AGAIN: WHAT DOES IT MATTER?

There are some further questions of considerable theological significance which arise from the whole subject of textual criticism of the NT. Here it will be possible to make only a few brief comments.

Can we recover the original text?

We have seen that scholars have with some confidence been able to trace early forms of the NT text back to the 2nd century. Some (such as the Alands) may speak with confidence of the original text. Comfort considers that several of the early papyri provide good evidence of a very early form of the text, not far removed from the original. Most are content to speak of the earliest recoverable form of the text. Whether this is identical with the original text is a vitally important question, but at present we do not have enough evidence to know. It would be exciting if more 2nd century papyrus MSS were discovered, or even some from the 1st century. This of course *could* happen but it is unrealistic to expect that it *must*, and we must be able to deal with the possibility that the earliest testimony to the NT text is only from the 2nd century. How then do we respond to this fact? Are we content to see this as early enough and close enough to the original NT text, or does it trouble us that the available evidence cannot be claimed with absolute certainty to be the original text?

Is it theologically important to recover the original text?

Does it matter if we do not have absolute certainty about the original text? Is it important? The statements of faith of some churches and Christian institutions refer to the biblical texts being inspired *in their original autographs*. This means that only the original text is considered to be inspired and so it becomes absolutely necessary to recover the original text. If this is seen to be impossible, where does that leave us? Do we now have a NT which is not inspired, or do we need to reopen the whole issue of inspiration, and especially the question of what form of the text we are willing to regard as inspired?

This in turn raises many other issues, not least the status of translations, which by definition are not the original autographs of texts written in Greek. Can a translation ever be considered the inspired word of God, and if so on what basis?

What text is "canonical"?

An understanding of the history of the NT canon and the process by which the different books came to be regarded first as scripture and then as members of a fixed list (canon) of such scriptural books raises questions about the canonical form of the text.

If we think of the canon as being finally decided in the 4th or 5th century, in which text form was it so decided? If the Byzantine text-type (or at least an early representative of the Byzantine text-type) was becoming dominant by that time, does that make the Byzantine text-type the canonical form, even if it is the latest text-type which we have? That is one possible conclusion.

But even if the 4th century marks a decisive stage in the history of the canon, we cannot think of that period in isolation. Books were regarded as scriptural and canonical in the 4th century only because of their prior acceptance (to a greater or lesser extent in different places) in the churches of the first three centuries. So the question then arises: in which text form or forms were the books accepted in those earlier years? If the answer is "in several different text forms", we realise that the issue of canonical form is far from simple.

Reflection on these several questions will perhaps make us aware that the theological position of the original autographs alone being inspired raises all sorts of practical difficulties. At the very least further consideration of these important questions is appropriate.

Questions for Reflection

1   Do we possess the original text of the New Testament?
2   Do we have satisfactory methods for restoring the original text?
3   Do uncertainties regarding the original text have any theological importance?
4   Can we speak of verbal inerrancy if we do not know what the original words were?
5   Does this situation destroy the doctrine of inspiration? What exactly can we say is inspired?

Chapter 19

EPILOGUE

We started this course with the hope and expectation of being better equipped to identify the original New Testament text in the midst of the many variants which have found their way into the witnesses over the centuries. Along the way we have discovered several obstacles. However the recovery of the original should always be our ultimate desire. We seek the precise wording of the original document for the sake of accurate exegesis, if for no other reason. A different version of a document may shed light on what a later scribe thought the text meant, but in order to know what the author meant we need the original words.

Some scholars have raised the issue of what it meant for a book to be published in ancient times. Publication then must have been different to what it is now. Presumably there was no such thing as a book launch with multiple authorised copies for sale and the author available to sign each one. However it is sometimes implied that there was really no publication at all and no release of an authorised version of a book. This must be questioned. At some point in time Paul sent his letter to the Romans, and Luke similarly sent his two-volume work to Theophilus. Ancient authors must have been aware of the damage which scribes could do to the original work, but that does not mean that they readily accepted scribal changes. If some time later you showed Paul two different MSS of Galatians, no doubt he was well able to say: this is what I wrote, not that. There is no reason to think that an ancient author was happier than a modern author for his or her words to be changed.

Nevertheless, even if our quest for the original remains the same, there are some problems, particularly in the area of methodology. We have seen that questions can be raised about each of the methods used over the past 150 years, whether the historical-genealogical method or thoroughgoing eclectism or reasoned eclecticism. Reasoned eclecticism is the common approach today, which, as we have observed, appears to be the most balanced, taking into account both external and internal factors, but just the same it involves too much subjective opinion to enable us to be absolutely sure of the results. Even if our preference is to put greater weight on the external evidence, we are left with the fact that our current state of knowledge allows us to identify only 2nd century forms of the text. That may be 90% or even 99% the same as the original, but at present we have no sure way of knowing.

Alongside these considerations, we can set the facts that the number of examples where there is serious uncertainty about the original text is quite small, and many examples come into the category of minor variations in wording which do not change the meaning of a passage. So we might well be content to say that we are close enough to the original to have confidence that what we read in UBS⁴ or UBS⁵ is substantially what the NT authors wanted to say. We can also be encouraged as we remember that the generally accepted form of the NT Greek text has remained quite stable from the time of Westcott and Hort until the present.

Furthermore, we recognise that the issue of variations in the text has never prevented the NT being accepted and used as scripture in the churches. Different forms of the text have been equally regarded as scripture. Each MS, we have suggested, was at some time someone's copy of the NT or some church's copy. Despite the many variants, there has never been a sense that we are dealing with different New Testaments or that this has produced different gospels or different basic beliefs. This principle applies to translations as well, both in ancient times and today. We still have the problem, if it really is a problem, of the use of different versions in our churches today, and yet we do not doubt that all believers, whatever Bible version they use, belong to the one family of God.

Perhaps we have finished this course on a different note to what we may have expected at the beginning. We cannot yet claim that we have the original wording of the NT. The quest to find the original is a worthy one and it continues. Yet the fact that we are left with unresolved questions is not the insuperable problem which we might have thought. In view of the small number of significant changes suggested in recent years, we may be closer to the original text than most textual critics are willing to claim, and in the meantime we can live with the variations. We can still use the NT, in the forms to which we currently have access, with confidence that we are reading what the authors, and indeed God himself, intended to communicate.

Appendix 1

GENERAL LIST OF GREEK MANUSCRIPTS

For the purpose of reference, a list of significant MSS is given here (papyri, uncials, and minuscules, but no lectionaries). The second column gives the date (sometimes the exact date, usually as century AD). The third column gives the Aland category, and the fourth column the text-type(s) identified by Metzger (either in *The Text of the New Testament* or in the *Textual Commentary*); here "P-Alex" = Proto- (or Primary) Alexandrian, "L-Alex" = Later (or Secondary) Alexandrian, and "Alex" alone means that Metzger has not specified. For the papyri, a description of the contents is also provided in the last column.

Cautionary comments have been made previously about the Alands' five categories. Nevertheless, as already stated, these categories have much practical usefulness. Detailed lists of papyri, uncials and minuscules are found in Aland, 96-162, with a select number of MSS of each type discussed in Metzger & Ehrman, 53-92.

See the further explanations and comments given at the end of this list.

Papyrus	Date	Aland	Metzger	Content
$\mathfrak{P}^1$	III	I		Portions of Matthew 1
$\mathfrak{P}^4$	III	I		Portions of Luke 1-6
$\mathfrak{P}^5$	III	I		Portions of John 1, 16, 20
$\mathfrak{P}^6$	IV	II		Portions of John 10, 11
$\mathfrak{P}^8$	IV	II		Portions of Acts 4-8
$\mathfrak{P}^{11}$	VI	I		Portions of 1 Corinthians 1-4, 6-7
$\mathfrak{P}^{13}$	III/IV	I		Portions of Hebrews 2, 10-12
$\mathfrak{P}^{14}$	VI	II		Portions of 1 Corinthians 1-3
$\mathfrak{P}^{15}$	III	I		1 Corinthians 7:18-8:4
$\mathfrak{P}^{16}$	III/IV	I		Portions of Philippians 3-4
$\mathfrak{P}^{19}$	IV/V	II		Matthew 10:32-11:5
$\mathfrak{P}^{20}$	III	I		James 2:19-3:9
$\mathfrak{P}^{22}$	III	I		Portions of John 15-16
$\mathfrak{P}^{23}$	III	I		James 1:10-12, 15-18
$\mathfrak{P}^{26}$	c 600	I		Romans 1:1-16
$\mathfrak{P}^{27}$	III	I		Portions of Romans 8-9
$\mathfrak{P}^{28}$	III	I		John 6:8-12, 17-22
$\mathfrak{P}^{29}$	III	I	West	Acts 26:7-8, 20

$\mathfrak{P}^{30}$	III	I		Portions of 1 & 2 Thessalonians
$\mathfrak{P}^{32}$	c 200	I		Titus 1:11-15, 2:3-8
$\mathfrak{P}^{33+58}$	VI	II		Portions of Acts 7, 15
$\mathfrak{P}^{34}$	VII	II		Portions of 1 & 2 Corinthians
$\mathfrak{P}^{37}$	III/IV	I		Matthew 26:19-52
$\mathfrak{P}^{38}$	c 300	IV	West	Acts 18:27-19:6, 19:12-16
$\mathfrak{P}^{40}$	III	I		Portions of Romans
$\mathfrak{P}^{44}$	VI/VII	II		Portions of Matthew & John
$\mathfrak{P}^{45}$	III	I	Caes; P-Alex (Acts)	Portions of all Gospels & Acts
$\mathfrak{P}^{46}$	c 200	I	P-Alex	Portions of Paul's Epistles (without 2 Thess, Philemon, Pastorals), plus Hebrews
$\mathfrak{P}^{47}$	III	I	L-Alex	Most of Revelation 9:10-17:2
$\mathfrak{P}^{48}$	III	IV	West	Acts 23:11-17, 25-29
$\mathfrak{P}^{49}$	III	I		Portions of Ephesians 4-5
$\mathfrak{P}^{50}$	IV/V	III		Acts 8:26-32, 10:26-31
$\mathfrak{P}^{51}$	c 400	II		Galatians 1:2-10, 13, 16-20
$\mathfrak{P}^{52}$	c 125	I		John 18:31-33, 37-38
$\mathfrak{P}^{53}$	III	I		Portions of Matthew & Acts
$\mathfrak{P}^{61}$	c 700	II		Portions of Paul's Epistles
$\mathfrak{P}^{64+67}$	c 200	I		Portions of Matthew 3, 5, 26
$\mathfrak{P}^{65}$	III	I		Portions of 1 Thessalonians 1-2
$\mathfrak{P}^{66}$	c 200	I	P-Alex	Large portions of John
$\mathfrak{P}^{69}$	III	IV		Luke 22:41, 45-48, 58-61
$\mathfrak{P}^{70}$	III	I		Portions of Matthew
$\mathfrak{P}^{72}$	III/IV	I	Alex	1 & 2 Peter, Jude
$\mathfrak{P}^{74}$	VII	I	Alex	Acts & large portions of Cath Ep
$\mathfrak{P}^{75}$	III	I	P-Alex	Portions of Luke & John
$\mathfrak{P}^{77}$	II/III	I		Matthew 23:30-39
$\mathfrak{P}^{81}$	IV	II		Portions of 1 Peter
$\mathfrak{P}^{85}$	IV/V	II		Portions of Revelation 9-10
$\mathfrak{P}^{90}$	II			John 18:36-19:7
$\mathfrak{P}^{91}$	III			Portions of Acts 2-3
$\mathfrak{P}^{92}$	III/IV			Portions of Eph & 2 Thess
$\mathfrak{P}^{99}$	IV			Portions of Paul's Epistles
$\mathfrak{P}^{100}$	III/IV			Portions of James 4-5
$\mathfrak{P}^{106}$	III			John 1:29-35, 40-46
$\mathfrak{P}^{115}$	III/IV			Portions of Acts 2-15
$\mathfrak{P}^{117}$	IV/V			Portions of 2 Corinthians 7
$\mathfrak{P}^{118}$	III			Portions of Romans 15-16
$\mathfrak{P}^{119}$	III			John 1:21-28, 38-44
$\mathfrak{P}^{120}$	IV			John 1:25-28, 33-38, 42-44
$\mathfrak{P}^{123}$	IV			Portions of 1 Corinthians 14-15

| $\mathfrak{P}^{124}$ | VI | | Portions of 2 Corinthians 11 |
| $\mathfrak{P}^{125}$ | III/IV | | 1 Peter 1:23-25, 2:1-5, 7-12 |

Uncial	Date	Aland	Metzger
א (Sinaiticus) (01)	IV	I	P-Alex; West (Jn 1:1-8:38)
A (Alexandrinus) (02)	V	III & V Gospels; I elsewhere	Byz (Gospels); Alex (elsewhere)
B (Vaticanus) (03)	IV	I	P-Alex
C (Ephraemi Rescriptus) (04)	V	II	L-Alex (?)
D Gospels & Acts (Bezae) (05)	V	IV	West
D Paul (Claromontanus) (06)	VI	III	West
E Gospels (07)	VIII	V	Byz
E Acts (08)	VI	II	West
F Gospels (09)	IX	V	Byz
F Paul (010)	IX	II	West
G Gospels (011)	IX	V	Byz
G Paul (012)	IX	III	West
H Gospels (013)	IX	V	Byz
H Acts (014)	IX	V	Byz
H Paul (015)	VI	III	Alex
I (016)	V	II	Alex
K Gospels (017)	IX	V	Byz
K Paul & Cath Ep (018)	IX	V	Byz
L (Regius) (019)	VIII	II	L-Alex (Gospels); Byz (elsewhere)
M (021)	IX	V	
N (022)	VI	V	Byz
P Gospels (024)	VI	V	Byz
P Acts, Paul, Cath Ep (025)	IX	V Acts, Rev; III elsewhere	Byz
S (028)	949	V	Byz
T (029)	V	II	L-Alex
V (031)	IX	V	Byz
W (032)	IV/V	III	L-Alex (Lk 1:1-8:12, Jn); Byz (Mt, Lk 8:13-24:53); West (Mk 1:1-5:30); Caes (Mk 5:31-16:20)
X (033)	X	V	L-Alex (?)

Z (035)	VI	III	L-Alex
Γ (036)	X	III	
Δ (037)	IX	III	L-Alex
Θ (Koridethi) (038)	IX	II	Caes
Λ (039)	IX	V	
Ξ (Zacynthius) (040)	VI	III	L-Alex
Π (041)	IX	V	Byz
Σ (042)	VI	V	Byz
Φ (043)	VI	III	
Ψ (044)	IX/X	II Cath Ep; III elsewhere	L-Alex
Ω (045)	IX	V	Byz
046	X	V	Byz
047	VIII	V	
048	V	II	
049	IX	V	Byz
051	X	III	Byz
052	X	V	Byz
057	IV/V	I	
070	VI	III	
071	V/VI	II	
073	VI	II	
076	V/VI	II	
077	V	II	
081	VI	II	
083	VI/VII	II	
085	VI	II	
087	VI	II	
088	V/VI	II	
091	VI	II	
094	VI	II	
098	VII	I	
0102	VII	II	
0108	VII	II	
0111	VII	II	
0141	X	III	
0150	IX	III	
0155	IX	II	
0162	III/IV	I	
0171	c 300	IV	West
0177	X	II	
0181	IV/V	II	
0189	II/III	I	
0201	V	II	

0220	III	I	Alex
0223	VI	II	
0225	VI	II	
0232	V/VI	II	
0233	VIII	III	
0234	VIII	II	
0243	X	II	
0243	X	II ?	
0247	V/VI	II	
0250	VIII	III	
0270	IV/V	II	
0271	IX	II	
0274	V	II	

<u>Minuscule</u>	<u>Date</u>	<u>Aland</u>	<u>Metzger</u>
1	XII	III Gospels; V elsewhere	Caes
5	XIII/XIV	III Acts, Cath Ep, Paul; V Gospels	
13	XIII	III	Caes
28	XI	III Mark; V elsewhere	Caes
33	IX	II Gospels; I elsewhere	L-Alex
36	XII	II Acts; III Cath Ep	
81	1044	II	L-Alex
88	XII	III	
104	1087	V Acts, Rev; III elsewhere	L-Alex
157	c 1125	III	
180	XII	III Acts; V elsewhere	
205	XV	III Gospels, Rev; V elsewhere	
221	X		
225	1192		
249	XII		
256	XI/XII	II Paul; V elsewhere	
322	XV	II Cath Ep; V elsewhere	
323	XI	II Cath Ep;V elsewhere	
326	X	III	L-Alex
383	XIII		West
429	XIV	V Paul, Revelation; III elsewhere	
442	XII/XIII	II	
565	IX	III	Caes
579	XIII	II Mark, Luke	L-Alex
597	XIII	V	
614	XIII	III	West

629	XIV	III	
636	XV		
642	XIV/XV	III Cath Ep; V elsewhere	
700	XI	III	Caes
892	IX	II	L-Alex
918	XVI	III Cath Ep; V Paul	
1006	XI	II Revelation; V elsewhere	L-Alex (Rev)
1010	XII	V	
1067	XIV	II Cath Ep; V elsewhere	
1071	XII	III	
1175	X	I	
1241	XII	I Cath Ep; V Acts; III elsewhere	L-Alex
1243	XI	I Cath Ep; III elsewhere	
1253	XV		
1292	XIII	II Cath Ep; V elsewhere	
1333	XI		
1342	XIII/XIV	II Mark	
1409	XIV	II Acts, Cath Ep; V elsewhere	
1424	IX/X	III Mark; V elsewhere	
1448	XI/XII	III Cath Ep; V elsewhere	
1505	XII	II Paul; V Gospels	
1506	1320	II Paul; V Gospels	
1611	XII (X in NA)		
		II Revelation; III elsewhere	L-Alex (Rev)
1735	X	II Cath Ep; III elsewhere	
1739	X	I Cath Ep, Paul; II Acts	L-Alex
1841	IX/X	II Revelation; V elsewhere	
1852	XIII	II Cath Ep; V Revelation; III elsewhere	
1854	XI	II Revelation; V elsewhere	L-Alex (Rev)
1881	XIV	II	
1891	X	II Acts; V elsewhere	
1962	XI/XII	II	
2050	1107	II	
2053	XIII	I	L-Alex (Rev)
2062	XIII	I	
2127	XII	II Paul; V elsewhere	
2298	XI	II Cath Ep; V Paul; III elsewhere	
2318	XVIII		
2329	X	II	
2344	XI	I Cath Ep, Rev; III elsewhere	L-Alex (Rev)
2427	XIV	I	

2464	IX	II
2473	1634	
2492	XII/XIV	III Paul, Cath Ep; V elsewhere
2495	XIV/XV	II (?) Cath Ep; III elsewhere

Explanations and comments

1   This list includes all the Greek MSS in the list of witnesses in the introductory pages of *A Textual Commentary on the Greek New Testament*. In addition to these, all other MSS in Aland categories I and II are included, except for those with fewer than ten verses, and the additional MSS taken into consideration for the text of UBS⁵, if cited in the apparatus (see the list on page 56 above).

2   Any MS not included in this list which you find in the UBS apparatus can be assumed to be category III. Any reading in such a MS should be considered Byzantine unless it is also attested in earlier witnesses. You can check the Aland lists if you feel you need more precise information about these MSS.

3   MSS with fewer than ten verses are not included (except for those in the *Textual Commentary*). This is admittedly arbitrary but has been done simply to prevent the list becoming inconveniently long. It does not mean that such a MS is not a significant witness for a reading which it attests. Aland has details about any such MS.

4   The papyri have been given an Aland category only up to $\mathfrak{P}^{88}$. Papyri after $\mathfrak{P}^{88}$ which are dated 4th century or earlier have been included in the list. Even though we do not know what category they should be given, it is likely that any MS of this date contains a significant proportion of early readings.

5   Minuscules 1 and 13 are sometimes cited alone, but usually as f^1 and f^{13} (ie family 1 and family 13):
    Family 1 includes minuscules 1, 118 (XIII), 131 (XIV), 209 (XIV/XV), 1582 (AD 948/9) and others.
    Family 13 includes minuscules 13, 69 (XV), 124 (XI), 174 (AD 1052), 230 (AD 1013), 346 (XII), 543 (XII), 788 (XI), 826 (XII), 828 (XII), 983 (XII), 1689 (AD 1200?), 1709 (X or XII?) and others.

6   Though included in the list of Western witnesses for the book of Acts in the *Textual Commentary*, 383 is not listed in either UBS or NA and does not appear to be cited in the textual notes of either edition; its date is given in the supplementary list in the *Textual Commentary*.

7   Some MSS have gone through a process of correction, in some cases more than once. With the following uncials the superscript number refers to a *group* of correctors (not just one individual). This information is from NA^{28}, 59* (see also Aland, 108).

א (01) א^1 (4th-6th century), א^2 (from about 7th century), א^3 (12th century), א^c (not assigned to a group)

B (03) B^1 (same period as B), B^2 (6th/7th century), B^3 (13th century)

C (04) C^1 (same period as C), C^2 (about 6th century), C^3 (about 9th century)

D (05) D^1 (6th-7th century), D^2 (about 9th century), D^3 (12th century), D^c (later hand, not assigned to a group)

D (06) D^1 (7th century), D^2 (about 9th century), D^c (later hand, not assigned to a group)

Appendix 2

MANUSCRIPTS OF JOHN CITED IN UBS

This list is in part a repetition of the MSS in appendix 1, but with some additions relevant to John's Gospel and with other MSS omitted which do not contain any text of John. The MSS given here are those cited in the UBS apparatus, and so you will find this a convenient check list when dealing with textual questions in John's Gospel. Some other MSS with text of John are included, though not cited in the UBS apparatus.

Papyrus	Date	Aland	Metzger	Content (for John)
$\mathfrak{P}^5$	III	I		1:23-31, 33-40, 16:14-30, 20:11-17, 19-20, 22-25
$\mathfrak{P}^6$	IV	II		10:1-2, 4-7, 9-10, 11:1-8, 45-52
$\mathfrak{P}^{22}$	III	I		15:25-16:2, 16:21-32
$\mathfrak{P}^{28}$	III	I		6:8-12, 17-22
$\mathfrak{P}^{36}$	VI	III		3:14-18, 31-32, 34-35
$\mathfrak{P}^{39}$	III	I		8:14-22
$\mathfrak{P}^{44}$	VI/VII	II		9:3-4, 10:8-14, 12:16-18
$\mathfrak{P}^{45}$	III	I	Caes	10:7-25, 10:30-11:10, 11:18-36, 42-57
$\mathfrak{P}^{60}$	c 700	III	L-Alex	16:29-19:26
$\mathfrak{P}^{63}$	c 500	II	West	3:14-18, 4:9-10
$\mathfrak{P}^{66}$	c 200	I	P-Alex	1:1-6:11, 6:35-14:26, 14:29-30, 15:2-26, 16:2-4, 6-7, 16:10-20:20, 20:22-23, 20:25-21:9
$\mathfrak{P}^{75}$	III	I	P-Alex	1:1-11:45, 11:48-57, 12:3-13:1, 13:8-9, 14:8-30, 15:7-8
$\mathfrak{P}^{76}$	VI	III		4:9, 12
$\mathfrak{P}^{90}$	II			18:36-19:7
$\mathfrak{P}^{106}$	III			1:29-35, 40-46
$\mathfrak{P}^{119}$	III			1:21-28, 38-44
$\mathfrak{P}^{120}$	IV			1:25-28, 33-38, 42-44

Uncial	Date	Aland	Metzger
ℵ (Sinaiticus) (01)	IV	I	P-Alex; West in 1:1-8:38
A (Alexandrinus) (02)	V	III or V	Byz
B (Vaticanus) (03)	IV	I	P-Alex
C (Ephraemi Rescriptus) (04)	V	II	L-Alex (?)

D (Bezae) (05)	V	IV	West
E (07)	VIII	V	Byz
F (09)	IX	V	Byz
G (011)	IX	V	Byz
H (013)	IX	V	Byz
K (017)	IX	V	
L (Regius) (019)	VIII	II	L-Alex (Gospels)
M (021)	IX	V	Byz
N (022)	VI	V	Byz
P (024)	VI	V	Byz
Q (026)	V	V	
S (028)	949	V	Byz
T (029)	V	II	L-Alex
U (030)	IX	V	
V (031)	IX	V	
W (032)	IV/V	III	L-Alex
X (033)	X	V	
Y (034)	IX	V	
Γ (036)	X	V	
Δ (037)	IX	III	L-Alex
Θ (Koridethi) (038)	IX	II	Caes
Λ (039)	VI	III	L-Alex
Π (041)	IX	V	Byz
Ψ (044)	IX/X	III	
Ω (045)	IX	V	
047	VIII	V	
050	IX	III	
054	VIII	V	
055	XI		
060	VI	III	
063	IX	V	
065	VI	V	
068	V	III	
070	VI	III	
078	VI	III	
083	VI/VII	II	
086	VI	III	
087	VI	II	
091	VI	II	
0101	VIII	II	
0105	X	III	
0109	VII	III	
0114	VIII	II	
0127	VIII	III	

0141		X	III
0145		VII	III
0162		III/IV	I
0210		VII	III
0211		VII	V
0212		III	III
0216		V	III
0217		V	III
0218		V	III
0232		V/VI	II
0233		VIII	III
0234		VIII	II
0238		VIII	III
0250		VIII	III
0256		VIII	III
0260		VI	III
0273		IX	V

Minuscule	Date	Aland	Metzger
1	XII	III	Caes
13	XIII	III	Caes
28	XI	V ?	Caes
33	IX	II	L-Alex
69	XV	V	Caes
157	about 1125	III	
180	XII	V	
205	XV	III	
249			
565	IX	III	Caes
579	XIII		L-Alex
597	XIII	V	
700	XI	III	Caes
828	XII	III	
892	IX	II	L-Alex
1006	XI	V	L-Alex (Rev)
1010	XII	V	
1071	XII	III	
1241	XII	III	L-Alex
1243	XI	III	
1292	XIII	V	
1342	XIII/XIV		
1424	IX/X	V	
1505	XII	V	

Appendix 3

TEXTUAL DIFFERENCES IN UBS⁵ AND NA²⁸ COMPARED TO UBS⁴ AND NA²⁷

These changes are incorporated into UBS⁵ and NA²⁸ from the revised edition (2012) of the *Editio Critica Maior* for the catholic epistles of the NT. These are the only books where UBS⁵ and NA²⁸ have a text different from earlier editions. This list is taken from NA²⁸, 50*-51* (and, almost identically, UBS⁵, 3*-4*, where 1 Pet 2:25 is not included).

		NA²⁷ and UBS⁴	NA²⁸ and UBS⁵
James	1:20	οὐκ ἐργάζεται	οὐ κατεργάζεται
	2:3	ἐκεῖ ἢ κάθου	ἢ κάθου ἐκεῖ
	2:4	οὐ διεκρίθητε	καὶ οὐ διεκρίθητε
	2:15	λειπόμενοι	λειπόμενοι ὦσιν
	4:10	κυρίου	τοῦ κυρίου
1 Peter	1:6	λυπηθέντες	λυπηθέντας
	1:16	[ὅτι]	-
	1:16	[εἰμι]	-
	2:5	[τῷ]	-
	2:25	ἀλλά	ἀλλ᾽
	4:16	ὀνόματι	μέρει
	5:1	οὖν	τούς
	5:9	[τῷ]	-
	5:10	[Ἰησοῦ]	-
2 Peter	2:6	ἀσεβέ[σ]ιν	ἀσεβεῖν
	2:11	παρὰ κυρίου	παρὰ κυρίῳ
	2:15	καταλείποντες	καταλιπόντες
	2:18	ὀλίγως	ὄντως
	2:20	[ἡμῶν]	-
	3:6	δι᾽ ὧν	δι᾽ ὅν
	3:10	εὑρεθήσεται	οὐχ εὑρεθήσεται
	3:16	ἐπιστολαῖς	ταῖς ἐπιστολαῖς
	3:16	στρεβλοῦσιν	στρεβλώσουσιν
	3:18	[ἀμήν]	-
1 John	1:7	δέ	-
	3:7	τεκνία	παιδία
	5:10	ἐν ἑαυτῷ	ἐν αὐτῷ
	5:18	αὐτόν	ἑαυτόν

2 John	5	καινὴν γράφων σοι	γράφων σοι καινήν
	12	πεπληρωμένη ᾖ	ᾖ πεπληρωμένη
3 John	4	τῇ ἀληθείᾳ	ἀληθείᾳ
Jude	5	πάντα ὅτι [ὁ] κύριος ἅπαξ	ἅπαξ πάντα ὅτι Ἰησοῦς
	18	[ὅτι]	-
	18	[τοῦ]	-

THE TEXT OF EPHESIANS

This article by Graham Simpson was published in Siga Arles, Ashish Chrispal & Paul Mohan Raj (eds), *Biblical Theology and Missiological Education in Asia. Essays in Honour of the Rev. Dr. Brian C. Wintle* (Bangalore: Asia Theological Association, India; Theological Book Trust; Centre for Contemporary Christianity, 2005), pages 125-143.

oooOOOooo

I am honoured to have the opportunity to contribute this piece in honour of Brian Wintle, who has been colleague, teacher and friend since my first acquaintance with him at the Union Biblical Seminary in January 1978. Apart from other things it has been a joy to have had a common interest in New Testament studies, even if his own expertise far outstrips my own.

The discipline of New Testament textual criticism is very much alive and well, though this fact is sometimes well hidden. Commentaries and Bible translations do not always give an accurate picture of important textual matters, and the absence of this subject from the curriculum in south Asian Bible colleges and seminaries is noteworthy. We will return to some of these issues later.

For this article I have chosen to focus on the epistle to the Ephesians. This book is not notorious for its textual difficulties, though the following pages will reveal much more variation than a casual reader of the English Bible may expect. Dr Wintle's recent publication on Ephesians (co-authored with Ken Gnanakan in the Asia Bible Commentary series) has turned my attention to that epistle, and this, I trust, is sufficient justification for making Ephesians the particular focus of this article.

I   SOME INITIAL IMPRESSIONS

From the translations

Readers of the English Bible might receive the impression that there are few textual issues related to Ephesians. NIV, most notably, records a variant in just one passage, namely the omission in "some early manuscripts" of the words "in Ephesus" in 1:1.[1] The believer who uses the NIV would be justified in thinking that the text of Ephesians is quite firmly established. NRSV is more revealing, with fifteen passages noted in which variants occur (including 1:1). NKJV notes variants in fourteen passages, though these do not include 1:1; one passage is merely a question of different translations, and so the total is really thirteen. There are only four passages which NRSV and NKJV both mention. So if one were to go to the trouble of adding up the textual information provided by these three versions, one would find variants in 24 different passages.

From editions of the Greek text

Not surprisingly, editions of the New Testament in Greek provide a greater range of information about textual variants. The latest (fourth) edition of the United Bible Societies text provides textual information on variants in 35 passages, with the *Textual Commentary* (second edition), supposedly a companion volume to the edition of the text, covering a further seven passages (as well as giving a note on the subscription found at the end of the epistle in some witnesses).

The difference between NIV (one variant) and the UBS text, with commentary (42 variants), is already striking, but in fact we have only uncovered the tip of the iceberg. The Nestle-Aland text takes us a step further, with variants recorded for 156 passages, on average almost exactly one for each verse. It is interesting to note that there are four variants recorded in NKJV which are not included at all in NA, an indication no doubt that the NKJV readings in these places are regarded by modern textual critics as having absolutely no claim to serious consideration.

This variety of approaches to the recording of textual variants immediately reveals that we cannot put confidence in any single text or translation to provide us with a comprehensive picture of the textual variation. There are in fact many more variants than all the above mentioned texts and versions have recorded, and one does not expect a complete statement in manual editions (as distinct from from major critical editions or scholarly monographs). Nevertheless, the fact that such different pictures are presented by the five texts or translations mentioned here could be a cause for uncertainty. Each text or version in its different way is inviting the

---

[1]   Several abbreviations are used. For Bible translations NIV (New International Version), NRSV (New Revised Standard Version) and NKJV (New King James Version). For Greek texts and tools UBS (the United Bible Societies text), NA (the Nestle-Aland text) and TC (the *Textual Commentary* based on the UBS text).

reader to exercise trust in the editors or translators that an adequate text as well as adequate information about variants is being presented, but it is virtually impossible for one who is a layman in this area to make an informed judgment on these matters.

From the commentaries

There is no need for a comprehensive survey, but a glance at some recent commentaries is instructive.[2] Neither Andrew Lincoln nor Peter O'Brien give any consideration to the text in their introduction, and the word "text" is not listed in the index of either commentary. In the body of their commentaries, Lincoln discusses 45 passages and O'Brien 16. Apart from comments on 21 separate passages, John Muddiman has a brief section on the text at the end of his introduction, in which he gives attention to the issue of the influence of parallel passages in Ephesians and Colossians on the textual tradition and on the reliability or otherwise of $\mathfrak{P}^{46}$.

II   TEXTUAL VARIANTS IN EPHESIANS

We here seek to give an overview of the variants in Ephesians, mainly on the basis of the information in NA[27]'s textual apparatus. No attempt is made to evaluate the readings. Relevant passages are grouped according to the present writer's own classification; no doubt different classifications are possible, and some readings could be put in a different group. In these notes "usual" or "usually" means the majority of manuscripts in the passage under discussion.

Minor grammatical variations

1:17 – the form of the subjunctive verb (*may give*) is uncertain, and the manuscripts vary between δώῃ (usually) and δῷ (in a few cases).
1:20 – instead of the usual ἐν τοῖς ἐπουρανίοις (*in the heavenly realms*), some manuscripts have ἐν τοῖς οὐρανοῖς (*in the heavens*). In 3:15 there is variation between the usual plural οὐρανοῖς and the singular οὐρανῷ, and in 6:12 the phrase usually found, ἐν τοῖς ἐπουρανίοις, is omitted altogether in one manuscript.
2:7 – the noun πλοῦτος (*riches*) which is understood as neuter in most witnesses can also be understood as masculine, so that in the phrase *the incomparable riches* we have variation between τὸ ὑπερβάλλον πλοῦτος (neuter) and τὸν ὑπερβάλλοντα πλοῦτον (masculine).

---

2   Andrew Lincoln, Word Biblical Commentary, 1990; Peter O'Brien, Pillar New Testament Commentary, 1999; John Muddiman, Black's New Testament Commentaries, 2001.

4:18 – instead of the usual ἐσκοτωμένοι (from σκοτόω) we sometimes find ἐσκοτισμένοι (from σκοτίζω). These are different verbs meaning in the passive *to be darkened, become dark.*

4:22 – the noun *desires* is usually plural (ἐπιθυμίας) but sometimes singular (ἐπιθυμίαν). Conversely, *heart* in 5:19 is usually singular (καρδίᾳ) but sometimes plural (καρδίαις).

5:4 – there is considerable variation between καί (*and*) and ἤ (*or*) in three different places in this verse.

6:10 – the phrase translated *finally* is in most manuscripts expressed in the genitive case (τοῦ λοιποῦ) but sometimes in the accusative (τὸ λοιπόν).

6:10 – in the same verse there is a variation between the compound verb ἐνδυναμοῦσθε (*be strong*) and the simple form of the same verb δυναμοῦσθε (approximately the same meaning).

6:20 – the variation between ἐν αὐτῷ and αὐτό (without a preposition) seems to reflect different views as to whether the verb παρρησιάζομαι can have a direct object (the second variant) or requires a prepositional modifier (the first variant).

Different forms (tense, voice or mood) of the same verb

1:7 – the present tense ἔχομεν (*we have*) is usually found but sometimes the aorist ἔσχομεν (*we had*).

1:9 – there is a variation between the participle γνωρίσας (*having made known*) in most manuscripts and the infinitive γνωρίσαι (*to make known*) in a few. The sense implied by the participle is: *he lavished ... by making known.* The infinitive implies purpose: *he lavished ... in order to make known.* (NIV cuts the necessary link between verse 8 and verse 9.)

1:20 – the manuscripts vary between the aorist tense ἐνήργησεν (*he exerted*) and the perfect ἐνήργηκεν (*he has exerted*). A similar example is in 4:11, with variation between the aorist ἔδωκεν (*he gave*) and perfect δέδωκεν (*he has given*).

1:20 – in the same verse there is variation between the participle καθίσας (*having made him sit*) and the indicative ἐκάθισεν (*he made him sit*). The participle expresses a second way in which God's power has been exerted (by *raising ... and by seating*), whereas the indicative expresses a second action alongside *he exerted* (ie *he exerted ... and he seated him*). (Manuscripts here also vary between the inclusion or omission of the pronoun αὐτόν [*him*].)

3:3 – the usual reading is the aorist passive ἐγνωρίσθη (*the mystery was made known*) but the aorist active ἐγνώρισε (*he [God] made known the mystery*) is also found.

4:23-24 – in these two verses the infinitives ἀνανεοῦσθαι and ἐνδύσασθαι (*to be made new ... to put on*) are sometimes written as imperatives, ἀνανεοῦσθε and ἐνδύσασθε. It is worth noting that the pronunciation of αι and ε was identical in the early centuries of the Christian era.

5:17 – the participle συνιέντες is sometimes found instead of the imperative συνίετε. The difference here is whether there are two separate commands (reading the imperative form – *do not be ... but understand*) or whether there are two separate adjectives relating to the one command (reading the participle – *not foolish ... but understanding*).

Different verbs

1:11 – the most common reading ἐκληρώθημεν (*we were allotted; ... chosen*, NIV) is sometimes replaced by ἐκλήθημεν (*we were called*).

2:4 – instead of ἠγάπησεν (*with which he loved us*), ἠλέησεν is also found (*with which he had mercy on us*).

3:1 – most manuscripts have no verb, but some include either πρεσβεύω (*I am an ambassador*) or κεκαύχημαι (*I boast*) at the end of the verse.

3:13 – instead of ἐγκακεῖν some manuscripts have ἐκκακεῖν (both meaning *to be discouraged* or *to lose heart*).

4:19 – the usual reading is ἀπηλγηκότες (*having lost all sensitivity*), but some manuscripts have ἀπηλπικότες (*having lost all hope*).

5:14 – as well as the usual ἐπιφαύσει σοι ὁ Χριστός (*Christ will shine on you*) there is ἐπιψαύσεις τοῦ Χριστοῦ (*you will attain to Christ*).

6:17 – most manuscripts have the verb δέξασθε (*take*), but the verb is omitted altogether in a few manuscripts.

Variants involving nouns (included, omitted or changed)

1:7 – the usual χάριτος (*grace*) is once replaced by χρηστότητος (*goodness*).

2:1 – the usual ἁμαρτίαις (*sins*) is once replaced by ἐπιθυμίαις (*desires*).

2:5 – instead of the most common reading τοῖς παραπτώμασιν (*transgressions*), there is a range of alternatives: τοῖς σώμασιν (*bodies*), ταῖς ἁμαρτίαις or τῇ ἁμαρτίᾳ (*sins* or *sin*), τοῖς παραπτώμασιν καὶ ταῖς ἁμαρτίαις (*transgressions and sins*), ἐν τοῖς παραπτώμασιν καὶ ταῖς ἐπιθυμίαις (*in transgressions and desires*).

2:15 – one manuscript omits the phrase ἐν δόγμασιν (*in regulations*).

2:20 – most manuscripts have ἀκρογωνιαίου (translated *chief cornerstone* in NIV, with the word *stone* supplied from the context), but several manuscripts remove any uncertainty by adding the word λίθου (*stone*).

2:22 – instead of θεοῦ (*God*), one manuscript has κυρίου (*Lord*). Conversely, in 5:10 instead of κυρίῳ (*Lord*) some manuscripts have θεῷ (*God*). Similarly in 5:17, there is variation involving κυρίου (*Lord*), θεοῦ (*God*) and Χριστοῦ (*Christ*); and in 5:29 the options are Χριστός (*Christ*) and κύριος (*Lord*).

3:5 – the word ἀποστόλοις (*apostles*) is omitted in one manuscript.

3:8 – the word ἁγίων (*saints; God's people*, NIV) is sometimes omitted.

3:9 – the usual reading is οἰκονομία (*administration*), but an alternative is κοινωνία (*fellowship*). (This variant is not recorded in UBS⁴ or NA²⁷, but is mentioned in *TC*²; the reading κοινωνία is reflected in NKJV.)

3:11 – the reading in the Greek manuscripts is πρόθεσιν (*purpose*), but Clement of Alexandria provides evidence for the reading πρόγνωσιν (*foreknowledge*).

3:12 – most manuscripts read πεποιθήσει (*boldness*) but there is also a reading τῷ ἐλευθερωθῆναι (*being made free*). Note that NIV has given a rather free paraphrase of this verse, and it is not clear which words of NIV correspond to which words of the Greek text.

4:14 – most manuscripts have simply τῆς πλάνης (*deceit*) but one adds τοῦ διαβόλου (*of the devil*), with the final words literally translated *the scheming of the deceit of the devil*.

4:16 – instead of the usual μέρους (*part*) some manuscripts have μέλους (*member*).

5:9 – instead of the usual φωτός (*light*) some manuscripts have πνεύματος (*Spirit*).

5:17 – the usual θέλημα (*will*) is once replaced by φρόνημα (*mind*).

6:12 – instead of the phrase πρὸς τὰς ἀρχάς, πρὸς τὰς ἐξουσίας (*against the rulers, against the authorities*), one manuscript has πρὸς τὰς μεθοδίας (*against the schemes*).

6:12 – instead of the more common τοῦ σκότους τούτου (*this darkness*), several manuscripts have τοῦ σκότους τοῦ αἰῶνος τούτου (*the darkness of this age*).

6:19 – instead of the more common τὸ μυστήριον τοῦ εὐαγγελίου (*the mystery of the gospel*), a few manuscripts omit the last two words, ie simply *the mystery*.

6:23 – the usual ἀδελφοῖς (*brothers*) is once replaced by ἁγίοις (*saints*).

6:23 – the usual ἀγάπη (*love*) is once replaced by ἔλεος (*mercy*).

Change of preposition or preposition added or omitted

1:4 – the usual reading is ἐν αὐτῷ (*in him*, ie Christ), but a variant (without a preposition) is ἑαυτῷ (*for himself*).

1:6 – instead of the genitive relative pronoun ἧς (genitive because attracted to the case of the antecedent, *grace which* …), some manuscripts read ἐν ᾗ (as in NKJV, *grace, by which He made us accepted*).

1:10 – in the phrase *in heaven*, there is variation between ἐπί and ἐν.

2:5 – a few manuscripts add ἐν before τῷ Χριστῷ, with the effect of changing the sense from *made us alive with Christ* to *made us alive in Christ*.

3:8 – the same addition of ἐν is found not uncommonly before τοῖς ἔθνεσιν, thus changing *preach to the Gentiles* to *preach among the Gentiles*.

3:9 – the same preposition ἐν is usually included in the phrase ἐν τῷ θεῷ (*in God*), but is sometimes omitted (meaning *for God*?).

3:20 – instead of ὑπὲρ πάντα (*above all; more than all*, NIV), the preposition is sometimes omitted (*able to do all things*).

4:8 – the usual reading is τοῖς ἀνθρώποις (*to men*), but some manuscripts include a preposition, ἐν ἀνθρώποις (*among men*).

4:16 – instead of the usual reading κατ' ἐνεργείαν (*according to the working;* ... *does its work*, NIV), some manuscripts change the preposition κατά to the conjunction καί (ie καὶ ἐνεργείας), thus linking this noun with the preceding noun (*supply and working*). A similar variation (involving mostly the same manuscripts) is seen in 4:19 (ἐν πλεονεξίᾳ or καὶ πλεονεξίας), and in 4:24 (τῆς ἀληθείας or καὶ ἀληθείᾳ), though no preposition is involved in the last mentioned verse.

4:23 – instead of τῷ πνεύματι, some manuscripts read ἐν τῷ πνεύματι. The difference in sense is not immediately obvious; both could mean *in (the sphere of) the spirit* or *by the Spirit*.

5:19 – some manuscripts read ψαλμοῖς (*with psalms*), others ἐν ψαλμοῖς (*in psalms*), with no clear difference in sense.

5:19 – instead of τῇ καρδίᾳ ὑμῶν (*with your heart*), some manuscripts add the preposition ἐν (*in*) to either the singular or plural of the same noun.

5:31 – in the phrase *shall be joined to his wife*, there is variation between a prepositional phrase πρὸς τὴν γυναῖκα αὐτοῦ and a simple dative case τῇ γυναικὶ αὐτοῦ.

5:32 – very occasionally omission of the second εἰς (ie before τὴν ἐκκλησίαν, *church*).

6:16 – instead of the usual ἐν πᾶσιν, some manuscripts read ἐπὶ πᾶσιν. Both can mean *in addition to all this* (NIV), though the first could mean *in (the midst of) all these*.

Variations involving the definite article (ie "the")

2:8 – πίστεως (usually) or τῆς πίστεως, *faith*.

2:13 – τοῦ Χριστοῦ (usually) or Χριστοῦ, *Christ*.

2:21 – πᾶσα οἰκοδομή or πᾶσα ἡ οἰκοδομή. The first strictly speaking means *every building* (implying several separate buildings), but is usually interpreted as equivalent to the second, ie *the whole building*.

4:7 – ἡ χάρις or χάρις, *grace*.

4:15 – ἡ κεφαλή or κεφαλή, *head*; and in the same passage Χριστός and ὁ Χριστός, *Christ*.

4:26 – τῷ παροργισμῷ or παροργισμῷ, *anger*.

Variations involving pronouns

1:4 – variation between the personal pronoun αὐτῷ (also in this variant the preposition ἐν is included) and the reflexive pronoun ἑαυτῷ. The same sort of variation is seen in 1:9, 2:15, 2:16, 4:16 and 5:25.

1:9 – τὴν εὐδοκίαν αὐτοῦ or τὴν εὐδοκίαν. Other places involving the inclusion or omission of a genitive personal pronoun are 1:16, 1:18, 2:4, 3:6

and 5:25. Similar is 2:5, which however involves a relative pronoun used as a possessive.

1:13 – ὑμεῖς or ἡμεῖς, and in the same verse ὑμῶν or ἡμῶν. This interchange between the first and second person pronouns is not uncommon (caused mainly by the identity in pronunciation between η and υ). Other examples are 1:19, 2:3, 3:13, 4:32, 5:2 (twice) and 6:12.

1:14 – ὅ ἐστιν or ὅς ἐστιν (and in 5:5). The first (found in most manuscripts in both passages) is a stock phrase (equivalent in English to *that is*). The second seeks to bring the relative pronoun into a more direct relationship with its antecedent, in 1:14 to πνεύματι (which denotes a personal being, *the Spirit*, though grammatically the noun is neuter) and in 5:5 to πλεονέκτης, *greedy person*.

Descriptions of God or Jesus

1:1 – Jesus is described as Χριστοῦ Ἰησοῦ (*Christ Jesus*) in most manuscripts, sometimes as Ἰησοῦ Χριστοῦ (*Jesus Christ*).

1:3 – God is ὁ θεὸς καὶ πατὴρ τοῦ κυρίου ἡμῶν Ἰησοῦ Χριστοῦ (*the God and Father* ...) in most manuscripts, but in one manuscript the words καὶ πατήρ (*and Father*) are omitted.

1:6 – in a few manuscripts the final phrase ἐν τῷ ἠγαπημένῳ is expanded by the words υἱῷ αὐτοῦ, with the longer phrase meaning *in his beloved Son*.

1:11 – before the words τοῦ τὰ πάντα ἐνεργοῦντος (*him who works out everything* ...), several manuscripts have the words τοῦ θεοῦ (*God who works out everything* ...).

3:1 – instead of the usual τοῦ Χριστοῦ Ἰησοῦ (*the Christ Jesus*), some manuscripts have τοῦ Χριστοῦ (*the Christ*).

3:14 – over against the shorter description τὸν πατέρα (*the Father*), in several manuscripts God is described more fully as τὸν πατέρα τοῦ κυρίου ἡμῶν Ἰησοῦ Χριστοῦ (*the Father of our Lord Jesus Christ*).

4:13 – in the phrase τῆς ἐπιγνώσεως τοῦ υἱοῦ τοῦ θεοῦ, a few manuscripts omit τοῦ υἱοῦ, so that the reference is to the knowledge of God (the Father) rather than to the knowledge of the Son of God.

5:5 – whose kingdom is it? At least four variants occur: τοῦ Χριστοῦ καὶ θεοῦ (in most manuscripts), but also τοῦ θεοῦ and τοῦ θεοῦ καὶ Χριστοῦ and Χριστοῦ τοῦ θεοῦ. The alternatives are *of Christ and God* or *of God* or *of God and Christ* or *of God's Christ*.

5:20 – God is described in different manuscripts as τῷ θεῷ καὶ πατρί (*God and Father*) or τῷ πατρὶ καὶ θεῷ (*Father and God*). (*God the Father* in NIV and other English versions ignores the word καί.)

5:21 – the manuscripts provide several options for the genitive phrase following ἐν φόβῳ (*in the fear*): Χριστοῦ (*of Christ*) or Ἰησοῦ Χριστοῦ (*of Jesus Christ*) or κυρίου (*of the Lord*) or θεοῦ (*of God*). For other relevant references see previously the discussion of 2:22 under "Variants involving nouns".

Other variants of potential interest or significance

1:1 – the inclusion or omission of ἐν Ἐφέσῳ (*in Ephesus*) is the best known variant in Ephesians.

1:1 – in the same difficult portion, it is worth noting the following variants: one which adds πᾶσιν in front of τοῖς οὖσιν (*all who are*), and another (in one manuscript only) which omits all these (two or three) words.

2:15 – as well as the more common ἕνα καινὸν ἄνθρωπον (*one new man*), there are the variants ἕνα κοινὸν ἄνθρωπον (*one common man*) and ἕνα καὶ μόνον ἄνθρωπον (*one and only man*).

3:7 – the more common reading for the words *which was given* is the genitive τῆς δοθείσης (*the grace which was given*) but several manuscripts have the accusative τὴν δοθεῖσαν (*the gift which was given*).

3:9 – the variants involve the inclusion or omission of πάντας (*all people*): either φωτίσαι πάντας (*to make all people see*) or simply φωτίσαι (*to bring to light*).

3:19 – as well as ἵνα πληρωθῆτε εἰς πᾶν τὸ πλήρωμα τοῦ θεοῦ (*so that you may be filled into all the fullness of God*), another reading is ἵνα πληρωθῇ πᾶν τὸ πλήρωμα τοῦ θεοῦ (*so that all the fullness of God may be filled*). A variation on the second (in one manuscript only) also includes at the end εἰς ὑμᾶς (... *filled into you*).

4:15 – the more common reading is ἀληθεύοντες (*speaking the truth*) but a few manuscripts have ἀλήθειαν δὲ ποιοῦντες (*doing the truth*).

4:15 – in addition to readings which identify Christ as the head, ie κεφαλή, Χριστός (*Christ the head* – these nouns with or without the article in different manuscripts), there is a variant κεφαλὴ τοῦ Χριστοῦ (*the head of Christ*) in one manuscript.

4:30 – the usual reading is μὴ λυπεῖτε (*do not grieve*), but one manuscript omits the negative. Unless this is an unintended scribal error, the verb without the negative must be understood as indicative rather than imperative, with the translation *and you are grieving the Holy Spirit of God*.

5:19 – most manuscripts read ᾠδαῖς πνευματικαῖς (*spiritual songs*), but there is a variant ᾠδαῖς πνευματικαῖς ἐν χάριτι (*spiritual songs in gratitude*), while another has only the first word ᾠδαῖς (*songs*).

5:30 – as part of the description of the body of Christ, many manuscripts add the descriptive phrase ἐκ τῆς σαρκὸς καὶ τῶν ὀστέων αὐτοῦ (*of his flesh and bones*).

5:31 – the words καὶ προσκολληθήσεται πρὸς τὴν γυναῖκα αὐτοῦ (*and he shall cling to his wife*) are omitted in a small number of manuscripts.

III   THE SIGNIFICANCE OF THE VARIANTS

Some readers may have (understandably!) lacked the courage, energy or time to work through the list of variants presented on the previous pages. However, some useful purpose will have been achieved if the list has merely created an impression of the number and variety of the variants, a rather different impression than one receives simply by reading Ephesians in the NIV.

How significant are these variants? Naturally, most readers will be interested to know what is the original text. What did Paul actually write? This question is especially important to those who hold a high view of the inspiration of Scripture and who believe that the author's precise words require the closest possible scrutiny in order to discover God's message.

This does not appear to be an unreasonable desire, but for better or worse the matter is not as simple as one might hope. Textual critics are generally agreed that we are not at present in a position to recover the original text. The best we can hope for is the earliest recoverable form of the text, perhaps dating back to the second century AD.

Such a consensus might be seen to be in stark contrast to opposite impressions. One such impression is given by the commonly used editions of the Greek New Testament: the United Bible Societies text and the Nestle-Aland text. UBS[3] was published in 1975, and the text of NA[26], published in 1979, was brought into line with the UBS text. The same text is used in the latest editions of both (UBS[4] and NA[27]) and thus has been produced unchanged for nearly three decades. The editors comment on this situation. In the preface of UBS[4] we are told that "this should not be misunderstood to mean that the editors now consider the text as established" (page vi), and similarly we read in the introduction to NA[27]: "It should naturally be understood that this text is a working text ... : it is not to be considered as definitive" (page 2*). Such statements hidden in introductory comments can easily be overlooked by the average reader, and one suspects that even New Testament scholars can be tempted to ignore these things. Most of the current generation of New Testament scholars have used no other form of text on a day to day basis, and under these conditions it is almost impossible to avoid falling into the trap of regarding this text form as "the original New Testament" to all intents and purposes.

The commentaries on Ephesians seem to confirm this.[3] Earlier commentaries, such as Abbott's (1897) and Robinson's (1904), give much textual information and comment on the significance of variant readings. Despite the possible temptation to regard the then recently published work of Westcott and Hort as solving all textual problems, they continued to give serious attention to textual questions.

Coming to more recent times, Barth (1974) has a short section on the text in his introduction (pages 52-53). He cautions against the attitude of F.W. Beare, whom he quotes as saying: "The text of Eph. has been transmitted with exceptional fidelity. There are few variants of importance, and practically no instance in which the true text is in doubt." Barth lists a number of "important or well-attested variants" (footnote 217) and promises detailed comment in his NOTES. In several places, he says, "the variant readings … imply a change in meaning". Best (1998) also has some general comments about the text in his introduction (pages 93-94), and discusses textual variants at the appropriate points in the commentary.

Section I of this article has referred to other recent commentaries. Of the three mentioned there Andrew Lincoln (1990) provides the most (and most helpful) comment on textual matters, and Peter O'Brien (1999) the least. Dr O'Brien mentions only a relatively small number of variants. Perhaps more significant is the observation that in every instance his textual preference agrees with the UBS/NA text. There may be excellent reasons for this on a case by case basis, but it is hard nevertheless to avoid the conclusion that this text has become the new "received text" and that the level of textual uncertainty is downplayed. The danger is heightened by dependence on the *Textual Commentary* to justify textual decisions, inasmuch as this work is produced by the editors of the UBS text to justify their decisions. There is an obvious risk of circularity here.

Of course, the field of textual criticism is a highly specialised one, and the writer of commentaries can hardly be expected to be competent to make independent judgments. Under these circumstances it would be better in many places for the commentator to avoid making a final judgment, but rather to allow the possibility of uncertainty and to explain what meaning the text might have if a manuscript variant happened to be what the author originally wrote.

---

[3]   Commentaries mentioned here include those by T.K. Abbott (International Critical Commentary, 1897), J. Armitage Robinson (2nd edition, 1904), Markus Barth (Anchor Bible, 1974), and Ernest Best (International Critical Commentary, 1998). See also footnote 2.

Having made these comments, I need to come back to the Ephesians variants and ask whether there are reasons for reconsidering the issue of the original text, in the light of the trend in practice (if not in theory) to regard the UBS/NA text as original. No doubt for many of the variants listed earlier, the possibility of being part of the original text can be ruled out through the application of the normal external and internal text-critical criteria. But that is not the whole story.

In particular, it seems appropriate to give greater consideration to readings found in early witnesses, even if only in one, especially in the light of the currently preferred text-critical method of eclecticism. In one form, this approach is willing to allow the possibility of a reading found in only one late witness being the original (if good reasons can be produced for such a conclusion). This is an extreme form of eclecticism, but if this approach has any validity at all, it surely opens the door for a more serious consideration of some manuscripts. At the very least it is right to expect that an adequate explanation be found for early readings. Variations from the UBS/NA text found in $\mathfrak{P}^{46}$ in 1:1, 15, 2:4, 5, 15, 3:8, 19, 20, 4:11, 15, 16, 28, 30, 5:5, 9, 17, 19, 31, 6:12, 23 are perhaps particularly worthy of reconsideration. The same can be said for the readings of B in 1:3, 15, 20, 2:1, 5, 22, 3:5, 19, 4:9, 28, 32, 5:2, 6:1, 12, 19. These are not the only passages worth reviewing, nor are these two the only manuscripts worthy of further consideration. Nor in the least is this to suggest that these readings are necessarily original, but simply that they warrant consideration and at least a serious explanation as to how they arose. Beyond the passages mentioned, the reader can make his or her own observations regarding variants which might have interesting implications for exegesis.

Beyond the primary issue of the original text, there is the broader question of the significance of the variant readings in the history of the church. One needs to bear in mind that each and every manuscript was someone's or some church's copy of the New Testament (or part thereof), not just a volume stored on a library shelf for scholarly reference from time to time. What different meaning does a particular variant give to a passage? How would the users of that particular manuscript have understood Paul's meaning in that passage? It does not seem unreasonable to ask that the writers of a future large-scale commentaries on Ephesians (or any other New Testament book) might give greater and more consistent consideration to such questions than seems to have been given in some recent scholarship.[4]

---

4   Reference to recent scholarship in this context is not meant to include the new volumes of the International Critical Commentary, where as one would expect textual matters are given due attention. Unfortunately, this

A broader theological issue relates to the question of inspiration. Often inspiration is defined as attaching to a particular form of words (according to many doctrinal statements, the words of the autographs). But in the absence of the autographs, can we claim inspiration for the copies that remain, let alone the translations which we now use? Textual criticism should encourage a more careful definition of inspiration. Related to this is the question whether a change is necessarily an error. The manuscripts witness many changes, but are all these "errors"? Is it possible to accept different wording or phraseology if it conveys the same meaning? How may one distinguish between change and error? (I have recently written briefly on some of these matters, in "Inspiration and the Text of the New Testament", *UBS Journal*, March 2004.)

IV   THE SOUTH ASIAN THEOLOGICAL SCENE

As stressed several times, this essay has not been an attempt to provide answers to specific textual questions in Ephesians, but should rather be considered as an awareness-raising exercise. New Testament textual criticism seems to receive very little attention in south Asian curricula. Rumour has it (which I have no means of verifying) that at the MTh level, the only colleges in India where this subject has been recently taught in its own right are the South Asia Institute of Advanced Christian Studies (SAIACS) in Bangalore and the Union Biblical Seminary (UBS) in Pune. It is likely that it receives much less attention at the BD/MDiv level. It seems reasonable to suggest that this subject be given far greater prominence, especially (though not only) in colleges where a high view of Scripture is held. (To this end the present writer is hopeful of producing a handbook for students, adaptable for use at different levels.)

The student training for pastoral ministry needs to know something of the transmission of the New Testament, if only to make a sensible response to questions of different forms of the text in English or south Asian vernacular languages. It is not unreasonable for church members to expect their pastor to be able to justify the use of a particular version or the use of several versions equally. Practice in textual criticism can also sharpen exegetical skills, as a student is required to grapple with the different meanings suggested by different variants in a passage.

---

series of weighty and technical commentaries is much less likely to be used than some other commentaries.

CONCLUSION

In writing on this subject I have attempted to disturb the lethargy which can easily attach to the question of the New Testament text. A brief glance at modern translations and some of the commentaries illustrates how deep the lethargy may be. The list of (some of) the variant readings in Ephesians illustrates what a range of variants actually exists, probably to the surprise of many readers. And I have suggested that this subject is significant enough to occupy a much more central place in our training institutions.

Appendix 5

INSPIRATION AND THE TEXT OF THE
NEW TESTAMENT

This is a slightly edited form of an article by Graham Simpson originally published in the *UBS Journal* (an occasional publication of the Union Biblical Seminary, Pune, Maharashtra, India), 2.1 (March 2004), pages 16-22.

oooOOOooo

The Bible provides its own testimony to the fact of inspiration (2 Tim 3:16), and this is accepted among evangelical Christians as a fundamental belief. Though no statement regarding Scripture appears in the historic creeds (such as the Apostles' Creed and the Nicene Creed), the inspiration and therefore the authority of scripture is rightly seen as a necessary foundation of Christian belief. Without this we flounder in a world of subjectivity, where it seems that almost any and every view can be regarded as a valid expression of so-called Christian theology.

In the light of the statement of 2 Timothy 3:16 that "all scripture is inspired", this brief essay seeks to ask the question 'what scripture?', especially in relation to the New Testament. The focus is not on the canon of the New Testament, but on the text. Assuming the canonical status of the twenty-seven books printed in our Bibles I wish to ask, 'Which version of the text?'

This should not be understood as, 'What is the best translation of the Bible?' Nevertheless, this question reminds us that there are many different versions of the New Testament. This is obviously so in English, but it is true also, though to a lesser extent, of the vernacular languages of south Asia. Are all these versions equally inspired? Is any translation considered to be inspired simply because the translator or translators manage to find someone to publish it with the title 'New Testament' attached to it? Ordinary Christians tend to assume so, but can we justify this?

In looking at this issue I want to go back a few steps. Sometimes one comes across a statement of faith issued by a Christian denomination or a Bible college which professes belief in the inspiration of the books of the Bible *in the original autographs*. What is the significance of these words printed in italics? Why is it felt necessary to add this sort of qualification to an assertion of the Bible's inspiration?

The essential reason is that from the very beginning the text of the New Testament was altered as it was copied and transmitted in manuscript form. For us in the age of the printed page, it is almost impossible to imagine a situation in which no two copies of the 'same' book were ever likely to be identical. But before the invention of printing this was inevitably so. One only has to try to copy a few paragraphs from another book to realise that it is almost impossible to copy without making changes. If we are making a genuine effort to copy accurately, such changes will be accidental errors. This certainly happened in the copying of the New Testament manuscripts. But in addition to accidental changes, there is plenty of evidence that with the best of motives scribes also made deliberate changes, as they sought to correct what they perceived as errors in the manuscripts from which they copied.

All this is part of the fascinating subject of textual criticism, and the previous paragraph is nothing more than a very brief summary of the sorts of things that happened in the copying of manuscripts. The interested reader can obtain further information elsewhere (for example, in a book like *The Text of the New Testament* by B.M. Metzger and B.D. Ehrman). However, the important point for us here is to note that of the thousands of copies of the New Testament text preserved in manuscript form, no two copies are identical. In fact it is not too much to suggest that, assuming that the New Testament books were written in different places of the Mediterranean world and at different times of the first century, there has probably *never* been a single Christian who has had access to the originals (the autographs) of all twenty-seven books of the New Testament. From the earliest times, as books were copied, changes crept into the text. Even if these changes were few and of small significance, nevertheless they were changes. The text was not transmitted in its original form.

For several centuries now, New Testament textual scholars have examined the evidence of the manuscripts and have attempted to reconstruct the history of the transmission of the Greek text. As a result it has been possible to discern several 'text-types'. A text-type is a group of manuscripts which contain a similar type of text – not identical wording in each manuscript, because no two manuscripts are identical, but a type of text which is in a broad sense the same. The three main types about which there is general agreement are called the Alexandrian, the Western, and the Byzantine. Since the time of Westcott and Hort, famous English scholars of the mid to late nineteenth century, it has been recognised that the Byzantine text is the latest text-type, which developed no earlier than the fourth century AD, a revision of earlier forms of the text. On the other hand the Alexandrian and Western texts are considered to go back to the second century AD, much closer to the time when the New Testament books were written. Westcott and Hort considered that the Alexandrian text (which they called the 'Neutral' text) was nearly always an accurate representative of the original text, as can be seen in the title of their edition of the Greek New Testament – *The New Testament in the Original Greek*.

Textual scholars today are not as certain as Westcott and Hort seemed to be about the Alexandrian text. It is not doubted that it is an early and on the whole reliable text-type. However, the Western text-type is also known to be early, and both the Alexandrian and Western texts are now recognised to be revisions of earlier forms. Not enough is known about the historical processes to be able to state with assurance how these two text forms (Alexandrian and Western) originated. From what earlier manuscripts were the earliest Alexandrian and Western texts copied? What sorts of changes were made? How close to the original text are these two text-types? Discoveries of early papyri continue to be made (though these are usually fragments of books and certainly not copies of the entire New Testament). If enough early papyri come to light, answers to some of these questions may be possible. But in the absence of sufficient manuscript evidence, it is not at present possible to give answers to the questions we want to ask. As a result scholars now content themselves by speaking about the 'earliest available form of the New Testament text' rather than the 'original text'.

There is not only a problem with the original Greek text, but the issue of translation must also be considered. The need to translate the New Testament into other languages inevitably arose at an early stage. The earliest translations were into the ancient Latin and Syriac languages (for churches in the west and the east of the Mediterranean world respectively). A moment's reflection will reveal that once you have translated a document into another language you are no longer dealing with the original text. Even if the translation is accurate (and defining the 'accuracy' of a translation is by no means straightforward), it is still true that you do not have the original text. You do not have the word order or the grammatical forms of the original. If you have access to an interlinear Greek New Testament (where English equivalents are printed beneath each Greek word in a totally literal manner), you can easily discover that it is not *possible* to translate Greek into English by using the same word order or the grammatical forms of the Greek language. To attempt to do this will not produce an English translation, but merely a series of English words which would not make sense to a hearer if they were read aloud. A proper translation of Greek into English (and most probably into any other language also) involves rewriting the text. There is no alternative, if an

English reader is to understand what the writer was trying to say in the original language.

We are now in a better position to understand why statements of faith which refer to inspiration often contain the qualification *in the original autographs*. The compilers of such statements wish to assert the inspiration of Scripture, but evidently are reluctant to claim such inspiration for copies which contain changes, dare we even say 'mistakes'. One can appreciate such reluctance, but what does this say about virtually every Bible that any believer has ever used? If *only* the autographs were inspired, that means that no other form of the text is inspired. But the fact is that the only access we have to the New Testament is in other (non-original) forms of the text. Does that mean that the book we open and read as the 'Word of God' may not be the Word of God after all? If only the autographs are inspired, does that mean that the New International Version or the King James Version or any particular south Asian vernacular Bible is not inspired? To come back to our earlier question: what can we claim has the attribute of inspiration?

The dilemma which these considerations pose is immediately obvious. If only the autographs are inspired, what we read in church or for our private devotions is not inspired. (This is true even if we read the New Testament in Greek, when we remember that even our editions of the Greek text cannot be claimed as the 'original' text.) If that is the case, where is our source of authority? Does not the whole Christian faith then rest on a very uncertain foundation?

Perhaps it is necessary to reconsider the matter of inspiration, and to ask the question afresh, 'To what does the characteristic of inspiration attach?' Is it in fact only the autographs that are inspired? It often seems to be assumed that only a particular form of words can be inspired. But though Scripture testifies to the fact of inspiration, it does not define inspiration in precise terms. I am not here speaking about the mode by which inspiration is conveyed to a text, but what it is in the finished product which is inspired. It is worth considering the possibility that inspiration does not attach to the words in a narrow sense but to the message in a broader sense. Immediately some will object that this sort of approach is the 'thin edge of the wedge', the beginning of a process by which the authority of Scripture will be diminished and eventually destroyed. In order to maintain the full authority of the Bible as God's Word, some may say, we must maintain a doctrine of verbal inspiration (that is, inspiration of the words). This response seems reasonable enough, but this is the very issue. It is indeed based on reason, on logic ('theo-logic', if you like). It is not a response which Scripture requires of us.

The subject is one which warrants a much fuller treatment than this short essay can provide. However, there is one particularly interesting set of data which come from the New Testament itself, namely, the quotations of the Old Testament in the New Testament. It is clear that at times the New Testament writers were somewhat loose in their quotations of Old Testament texts. There are examples where the same text is quoted in different forms in different New Testament books. The command to honour one's father and mother (Exodus 20:12) is quoted in Matthew 15:4, Mark 7:10 and Ephesians 6:2, with slight variations in wording in all three passages. The differences are often minor, and may not even be seen in an English translation, but the point remains that the New Testament writers do not seem as fussy as we might wish them to be about precise wording. In Romans 9:33 and 1 Peter 2:6, Isaiah 28:16 is quoted; in the Romans passage Paul has replaced part of the Isaiah verse with words from another passage. It is particularly interesting when the same author quotes a particular passage in different forms, as Luke does in Luke 20:17 and Acts 4:11, quoting Psalm 118:2. Sometimes the wording of the Septuagint (the Greek translation of the Old Testament begun in the third century BC) is followed, in places where the Hebrew text is somewhat different, as in the epistle to the Hebrews (1:10-12, 3:15, 10:37-38 and elsewhere). This epistle, like many other New Testament books, contains a mixture of texts, sometimes following the Septuagint, sometimes a text closer to the Hebrew.

All this shows us that even in the period when the New Testament books were being written there were known to be different forms of the text of Scripture (in this case Old Testament Scripture). Authors of New Testament books do not seem embarrassed by this fact. The statement about the inspiration of Scripture in 2 Timothy 3:16 is written in this situation. Clearly the author did not consider that the existence of different forms of the same text ruled out the possibility of a doctrine of inspiration.

In the light of this we may claim that the New Testament doctrine of inspiration does not require that the actual original words of a scriptural document be preserved. The precise wording of passages cited as 'Scripture' (or with an introductory formula that clearly identifies the passage as Scripture) was of secondary importance. What seems to have been important was that the quotation which is given in any particular passage is an accurate representation of the sense of the Old Testament verse. If that is the New Testament's attitude to Old Testament Scripture, there seems to be no reason to prevent a similar approach to the New Testament books. What is inspired is not the words but the sense. Words are needed to convey the sense, but the sense may be conveyed in more than one form of words. To put it differently, more than one form of words may be considered 'inspired'.

Whatever view of inspiration is held in theory, what is outlined above is in practice the attitude of most Christians anyway. Every preacher and pastor knows the inconvenience of the members of their congregation having different versions of the Bible. But we do not object theologically to this practice. We sit in Bible study groups with the leader using (perhaps) the NIV, with different members of the group sharing what their own version says (perhaps RSV, NRSV, Good News Bible, Living Bible, Amplified Bible, or a number of others). No one objects by saying, 'That's not what the Bible says!' We are happy to accept any translation as being 'what the Bible says'. In practice we accept a variety of forms of the text as being inspired, certainly not only the autographs of the various books.

Does this means that any translation can claim to be inspired? That conclusion is more than the argument of this essay would support. In any case, if what has been said above is right, it is not a particular version which is inspired but the message contained in the translation. One may suggest with some confidence that a translation made by a scholar or group of scholars who can claim some competence in both the source language (in this case Greek) and the target language (English or whatever other language) can reasonably claim to convey the message which God intended when he inspired the several books of Scripture in the first place. Furthermore one might also suggest that texts which have been produced with less competence than might be desired can also claim to communicate the inspired message. Many manuscripts down through the ages have been copied by scribes who have had minimal competence, and have been found to contain numerous errors as well as deliberate alterations. However, even in this case, unless a manuscript has been so corrupted as to be completely misleading (and the present author is not aware of any manuscript which can be so described), it would seem reasonable to suggest that a sincere seeker after the truth would not fail to find the truth in spite of the relatively poor quality of the text which he or she is using.

At least one branch of modern Christianity seeks to bypass this whole question by claiming one form of the text as original and inspired. There is an apparently growing support in certain evangelical (or perhaps better fundamentalist) circles for the so-called Majority Text, the text contained in the bulk of extant New Testament manuscripts and representing the Byzantine text-type. Proponents of this view hold as a virtual tenet of faith that this form of the text (best known to us in the King James Version of 1611) existed from the earliest days, and that it is an accident of history that early copies of this text no longer exist, the result, they claim, of the manuscripts wearing out through overuse.

This view may seem a very convenient solution, but in fact it fails to solve some major problems. First, the opinion that the Byzantine text-type was the original text of which no copies happen to have survived is nothing more than speculation; there is not a scrap of evidence in its favour, and much evidence pointing in the opposite direction. Secondly, even when we look at the manuscripts that represent the Byzantine text-type, we do not find a uniform text; though the Byzantine manuscripts have a common type of text they also contain many variations (as do all Greek manuscripts known to us). Thirdly, when we come to the King James Version, it is based on a quite inferior form of the Byzantine text-type, the result of the accidents of history related to the printing of the first editions of the Greek New Testament early in the sixteenth century. And fourthly, there is no avoiding the fact that the King James Version is a translation, affected by the factors that apply to any translation from one language into another; the English of the King James Version is not the original text.

Significant difficulties attach to any view of inspiration which limits inspiration to the wording of the now lost autographs. But perhaps it is not necessary to maintain such a view. Perhaps inspiration can be defined in other terms, more broadly than has usually been done, with inspiration regarded as attaching to the *message* of Scripture rather than its specific words.

LIST OF RESOURCES

Following most entries a *New Testament Abstracts* reference is provided in square brackets [volume number plus item or page number]. The *NTA* abstract provides a helpful summary for material which is not otherwise accessible. Names of journals are abbreviated as in *NTA*. Several articles from the online journal *TC: A Journal of Biblical Textual Criticism* (http: // purl.org / TC) have been included.

Abbreviations used in this book

Aland	K. Aland & B. Aland, *The Text of the New Testament: An Introduction to the Critical Editions and to the Theory and Practice of Modern Textual Criticism*, 2nd edition, translated by E.F. Rhodes, Grand Rapids: Eerdmans, 1989 [34, p 234]
Black	D.A. Black (ed), *Rethinking New Testament Textual Criticism*, Grand Rapids: Baker, 2002 [47, p 141]
Comfort	P. Comfort, *Encountering the Manuscripts: An Introduction to New Testament Paleography & Textual Criticism*, Nashville: Broadman & Holman, 2005
Ehrman & Holmes	B.D. Ehrman & M.W. Holmes, *The Text of the New Testament in Contemporary Research: Essays on the Status Quaestionis*, Grand Rapids: Eerdmans, 1995 [40, p 136]
Epp & Fee	E.J. Epp & G.D. Fee, *Studies in the Theory and Method of New Testament Textual Criticism*, Grand Rapids: Eerdmans, 1993 [38, p 276]
Metzger & Ehrman	B.M. Metzger & B.D. Ehrman, *The Text of the New Testament: Its Transmission, Corruption and Restoration*, 4th edition, New York: Oxford University Press, 2005 [50, p 154]
Textual Commentary	B.M. Metzger, *A Textual Commentary on the Greek New Testament*, 2nd edition, New York: United Bible Societies, 1994 [39, p 495]

Standard introductions

B.M. Metzger & B.D. Ehrman, *The Text of the New Testament: Its Transmission, Corruption and Restoration*, 4th edition, New York: Oxford University Press, 2005 [50, p 154]

K. Aland & B. Aland, *The Text of the New Testament: An Introduction to the Critical Editions and to the Theory and Practice of Modern Textual Criticism*, 2nd edition, translated by E.F. Rhodes, Grand Rapids: Eerdmans, 1989 [34, p 234]

Other introductions

D.A. Black, *New Testament Textual Criticism: A Concise Guide*, Grand Rapids: Baker, 1996 [38, p 444]

D.A. Black (ed), *Rethinking New Testament Textual Criticism*, Grand Rapids: Baker, 2002 [47, p 141]

P. Comfort, *Encountering the Manuscripts: An Introduction to New Testament Paleography & Textual Criticism*, Nashville: Broadman & Holman, 2005

P.W. Comfort, *The Quest for the Original Text of the New Testament*, Grand Rapids: Baker, 1992 [37, p 264]

J.K. Elliott & I. Moir, *Manuscripts and the Text of the New Testament. An Introduction for English Readers*, Edinburgh: T & T Clark, 1995 [40, p 509]

J.H. Greenlee, *Scribes, Scrolls, and Scripture. A Student's Guide to New Testament Textual Criticism*, Grand Rapids: Eerdmans, 1985 [31, p 219]

J. Harold Greenlee, *Introduction to New Testament Textual Criticism*, Grand Rapids, Michigan: Eerdmans, 1983, rev edition 1995 [40, p 129]

J. Harold Greenlee, *The Text of the New Testament: From Manuscript to Modern Edition*, Peabody: Hendrickson, 2008 [53, p 150]

R.F. Hull, *The Story of the New Testament Text. Movers, Materials, Motives, Methods, and Models*, Atlanta: Society of Biblical Literature, 2010 [55, p 362]

D.C. Parker, *An Introduction to the New Testament Manuscripts and Their Texts*, Cambridge: Cambridge University Press, 2008 [53, p 378]

L. Vaganay, *An Introduction to New Testament Textual Criticism*, 2nd edition, Cambridge & New York: Cambridge University Press, 1991 [36, p 417]

P.D. Wegner, *A Student's Guide to Textual Criticism of the Bible*, Downers Grove: IVP, 2006 [50, p 584]

Commentaries

P.W. Comfort, *New Testament Text and Translation Commentary*, Carol Stream: Tyndale, 2008

B.M. Metzger, *A Textual Commentary on the Greek New Testament*, 2nd edition, New York: United Bible Societies, 1994 [39, p 495]

General survey articles

P.W. Comfort, "Textual Criticism", in *Dictionary of the Later New Testament and Its Developments*, Downers Grove: InterVarsity Press, 1997

D.T. Ejenobo, "Textual Criticism: Its Value to New Testament Studies", *AsiaJournTheol* 22 (2008), 126-141 [53 # 88]

B.D. Ehrman, "Textual Criticism", in J.B. Green (ed), *Hearing the New Testament: Strategies for Interpretation*, Grand Rapids: Eerdmans, 1995

E.J. Epp, "Textual Criticism in the Exegesis of the New Testament, with an Excursus on Canon", in S.E. Porter (ed), *A Handbook to the Exegesis of the New Testament*, Leiden: Brill, 1997

G.D. Fee, "Textual Criticism", in *Dictionary of Jesus and the Gospels*, Downers Grove: InterVarsity Press, 1992

M. Holmes, "Textual Criticism", in D.A. Black & D.S. Dockery (ed), *New Testament Criticism and Interpretation*, Grand Rapids: Zondervan, 1991

M.W. Holmes, "Textual Criticism", in *Dictionary of Paul and His Letters*, Downers Grove: InterVarsity Press, 1993

S.E. Porter, "Textual Criticism", in *Dictionary of New Testament Background*, Downers Grove: Inter Varsity Press, 2000

E.J. Schnabel, "Textual Criticism: Recent Developments", in S. McKnight & G.R. Osborne (ed), *The Face of New Testament Studies: A Survey of Recent Research*, Grand Rapids: Baker, 2004

More detailed studies

B. Aland & J. Delobel (ed), *New Testament Textual Criticism, Exegesis, and Early Church History. A Discussion of Methods*, Kampen: Kok Pharos, 1994 [39, p 490]

C.-B. Amphoux & J.K. Elliott (ed), *The New Testament Text in Early Christianity. Proceedings of the Lille Colloquium, July 2000*, Lausanne: Éditions du Zèbre, 2003 [49, p 151]

J.N. Birdsall, *Collected Papers in Greek and Georgian Textual Criticism*, Piscataway: Gorgias, 2006 [51, p 145]

D.A. Black (ed), *Scribes and Scripture. New Testament Essays in Honor of J. Harold Greenlee*, Winona Lake: Eisenbrauns, 1992 [37, p 433]

J.W. Childers & D.C. Parker (ed), *Transmission and Reception: New Testament Text-Critical and Exegetical Studies*, Piscataway: Gorgias, 2006 [51, p 147]

A. Denaux (ed), *New Testament Textual Criticism and Exegesis. Festschrift J. Delobel*, Leuven: Leuven University Press & Peeters, 2002 [46, p 547]

P. Doble & J. Kloha (ed), *Texts and Traditions: Essays in Honour of J. Keith Elliott*, Leiden & Boston: Brill, 2014 [59, p 136]

B.D. Ehrman, *Studies in the Textual Criticism of the New Testament*, Leiden & Boston: Brill, 2006 [51, p 149]

B.D. Ehrman & M.W. Holmes, *The Text of the New Testament in Contemporary Research: Essays on the* Status Quaestionis, Grand Rapids: Eerdmans, 1995 [40, p 136]

J.K. Elliott (ed), *Studies in New Testament Language and Text. Essays in Honour of George D. Kilpatrick on the Occasion of his sixty-fifth Birthday*, Leiden: Brill, 1976 [21, p 80]

J.K. Elliott, *Essays and Studies in New Testament Textual Criticism*, Córdoba: Ediciónes El Almendro, 1992 {37, p 105]

E.J. Epp & G.D. Fee, *New Testament Textual Criticism. Its Significance for Exegesis. Essays in Honour of Bruce M. Metzger*, New York & Oxford: Clarendon, 1981 [27, p 88]

E.J. Epp & G.D. Fee, *Studies in the Theory and Method of New Testament Textual Criticism*, Grand Rapids: Eerdmans, 1993 [38, p 276]

E.J. Epp, *Perspectives on New Testament Textual Criticism. Collected Essays, 1962-2004*, Leiden: Brill, 2005 [50, p 150]

C.E. Hill & M.J. Kruger (ed), *The Early Text of the New Testament*, Oxford & New York: Oxford University Press, 2012 [57, p 155]

S. McKendrick & O.A. O'Sullivan (ed), *The Bible as Book. The Transmission of the Greek Text*, New Castle: Oak Knoll, 2003 [48, p 604]

B.M. Metzger, *The Early Versions of the New Testament: Their Origin, Transmission and Limitations*, Oxford: Clarendon Press, 1977 [22, p 83]

D.C. Parker, *Manuscripts, Texts, Theology. Collected Papers 1977-2007*, Berlin & New York: de Gruyter, 2009 [54, p 150]

D.C. Parker, *Textual Scholarship and the Making of the New Testament*, Oxford & New York: Oxford University Press, 2012 [59, p 143]

S.E. Porter & M.J. Boda (ed), *Translating the New Testament. Text, Translation, Theology*, Grand Rapids & Cambridge: Eerdmans, 2009 [54, p 150]

S.E. Porter & C.A. Evans (ed), *New Testament Text and Language. A Sheffield Reader*, Sheffield: Sheffield Academic Press, 1997 [41, p 540]

K. Wachtel & M.W. Holmes (ed), *The Textual History of the Greek New Testament. Changing Views in Contemporary Research*, Atlanta: Society of Biblical Literature, 2011 [56, p 389]

W. Weren & D.-A. Koch (ed), *Recent Developments in Textual Criticism. New Testament, Other Early Christian and Jewish Literature. Papers Read at a NOSTER Conference in Münster, January 4-6, 2001*, Assen: Van Gorcum, 2003 [48, p 406]

B.F. Westcott & F.J.A. Hort, *Introduction to the New Testament in the Original Greek*, New York: Harper & Brothers, 1882 (1988 reprint) [33, p 241]

Methodology

C.S. Baldwin, *The So-Called Mixed Text. An Examination of the Non-Alexandrian and Non-Byzantine Text-Type in the Catholic Epistles*, New York & Bern: Lang, 2011 [57, p 621]

J.N. Birdsall, "A hundred years and more since Westcott and Hort: where have we got to in the textual criticism of the New Testament?" *ProclrBibAssoc* 16 (1993), 7-19 [39 # 678]

M. Black & R. Davidson, *Constantin von Tischendorf and The Greek New Testament*, Glasgow: University of Glasgow Press, 1981 [26, p 189]

C. Caragounis, "The Impact of the Historical Greek Pronunciation on the Transmission of the New Testament Text", chapter 8 (pp 475-564) of *The Development of Greek and the New Testament*, Grand Rapids: Baker, 2006 (corrected edition)

S. Carlson, "Comments on the Coherence-Based Genealogical Method", *TC: A Journal of Biblical Textual Criticism* 20 (2015)

T.S. Caulley, "The 'New' Textual Criticism: Challenges and Promise", *Stone-Campbell Journal* 13 (2010), 225-241 [55 # 823]

J. Delobel, "Focus on the 'Western' Text in Recent Studies", *EphTheol Lov* 73 (1997), 401-410 [42 # 1560]

B.D. Ehrman, "Methodological Developments in the Analysis and Classification of New Testament Documentary Evidence", *NovTest* 29 (1987), 22-45 [31 # 978]

B.D. Ehrman, "The Use of Group Profiles for the Classification of New Testament Documentary Evidence", *JournBibLit* 106 (1987), 465-486 [32 # 523]

B.D. Ehrman, "A Problem of Textual Circularity: The Alands on the Classification of New Testament Manuscripts", *Biblica* 70 (1989), 377-388 [34 # 553]

B.D. Ehrman, *The Orthodox Corruption of Scripture. The Effect of Early Christological Controversies on the Text of the New Testament*, 2nd edition, Oxford & New York: Oxford University Press, 2011 [56, p 153; for 1st edition, see 38, p 112]

J.K. Elliott, "In Defence of Thoroughgoing Eclecticism In New Testament Textual Criticism", *RestorQuart* 21 (1978), 95-115 [22 # 701]

J.K. Elliott, "Keeping up with Recent Studies. XV. New Testament Textual Criticism", *ExpTimes* 99 (1987), 40-45 [32 # 524]

J.K. Elliott, "The Aorist Middle of ἀποκρίνομαι", *ZeitNTWiss* 96 (2005), 126-128 [49 # 1563]

J.K. Elliott, *New Testament Textual Criticism. The Application of Thoroughgoing Principles. Essays on Manuscripts and Textual Variation*, Leiden & Boston: Brill, 2010 [55, p 359]

E.J. Epp, "The Twentieth Century Interlude In New Testament Textual Criticism", *JournBibLit* 93 (1974), 386-414

E.J. Epp, "The Eclectic Method in New Testament Textual Criticism: Solution or Symptom?" *HarvTheol Rev* 69 (1976), 211-256 [22 # 339]

E.J. Epp, "New Testament Textual Criticism in America: Requiem for a Discipline", *JournBibLit* (1979), 94-98 [24 # 27]

E.J. Epp, "A Continuing Interlude in New Testament Textual Criticism?" *HarvTheolRev* 73 (1980), 131-151 [25 # 402]

E.J. Epp, "New Testament Textual Criticism Past, Present, and Future: Reflections on the Alands' *Text of the New Testament*", *HarvTheolRev* 82 (1989), 213-229 [34 # 54r]

E.J. Epp, "Why Does New Testament Textual Criticism Matter? Refined Definitions and Fresh Directions", *ExpTimes* 125 (2014), 417-431 [59 # 44]

G. Gäbel et al, "The CBGM Applied to Variants from Acts: Methodological Background", *TC: A Journal of Biblical Textual Criticism* 20 (2015)

H. Gamble, Jr., *The Textual History of the Letter to the Romans. A Study in Textual and Literary Criticism*, Grand Rapids: Eerdmans, 1977 [21, p 337]

W.M.A. Hendriks, "Brevior lectio praeferenda est verbosiori", *RevBib* 112 (2005), 567-595 [50 # 1566]

W. Hendriks, "Internal Evidence of Readings", *EstBib* 69 (2011), 301-322 [56 # 1580]

W. Hendriks, "The Case for the Primacy of the Western Text", *EstBib* 72 (2014), 411-436 [59 # 45]

H.A.G. Houghton, "Recent Developments in New Testament Textual Criticism", *EarlyChrist* 2 (2011), 245-258 [56 # 93]

A. Hüffmeier, "The CBGM Applied to Variants from Acts", *TC: A Journal of Biblical Textual Criticism* 20 (2015)

B.L.F. Kampuis et al, "Sleepy Scribes and Clever Critics: A Classification of Conjectures on the Text of the New Testament", *NovTest* 57 (2015), 72-90 [59 # 47]

G.D. Kilpatrick, "Some thoughts on modern textual Criticism and the synoptic Gospels", *NovTest* 19 (1977), 275-292 [23 # 39]

G.D. Kilpatrick, "Text and Language in the Greek New Testament", *Classical Bulletin* 64 (1988), 71-72 [33 # 1045]

G.D. Kilpatrick, *The Principles and Practice of New Testament Textual Criticism. Collected Essays of G.D. Kilpatrick*, Leuven: Leuven University Press, 1990 [35, p 233]

J. Krans, *Beyond What Is Written. Erasmus and Beza as Conjectural Critics of the New Testament*, Leiden & Boston: Brill, 2006 [51, p 153]

C. Landon, *A Text-Critical Study of the Epistle of Jude*, Sheffield: Sheffield Academic Press, 1996 [41, p 375]

M.W. Martin, "Defending the 'Western Non-Interpolations': The Case for an Anti-Separationist *Tendenz* in the Longer Alexandrian Readings", *JournBibLit* 124 (2005), 269-294 [50 # 68]

B.M. Metzger, "The Westcott and Hort Greek New Testament – Yesterday and Today", *Cambridge Review* (20 Nov 1981), 71-76 [26 # 411]

J. Miller, "(Mis)understanding Westcott and Hort", *RestorQuart* 41 (1999), 155-162 [44 # 60]

J.D. Miller, "The Long and Short of *Lectio Brevior Potior*", *BibTrans* 57 (2006), 11-16 [50 # 836]

I.A. Moir, "A Mini-Guide to New Testament Textual Criticism", *BibTrans* 36 (1985), 122-129 [29 # 864]

R.L. Omanson, "A Perspective on the Study of the New Testament Text", *BibTrans* 34 (1983), 107-122 [27 # 861]

F. Pack, "One Hundred Years since Westcott and Hort: 1881-1981", *Restor Quart* 26 (1983), 65-79 [28 # 861]

D.C. Parker, "The Development of Textual Criticism since B.H. Streeter", *NTStud* 24 (1977), 149-162 [22 # 341]

D.C. Parker & H.A.G. Houghton (ed), *Textual Variation: Theological and Social Tendencies? Papers from the Fifth Birmingham Colloquium on the Textual Criticism of the New Testament*, Piscataway: Gorgias, 2008 [53, p 378]

G.A. Patrick, "1881-1981: The Centenary of the Westcott and Hort Text", *ExpTimes* 92 (1981), 359-364 [26 # 412]

J.H. Petzer, "A survey of the developments in the textual criticism of the Greek New Testament since UBS³", *Neotestamentica* 24 (1990), 71-92 [35 # 540]

J.H. Petzer, "Author's style and the textual criticism of the New Testament", *Neotestamentica* 24 (1990), 185-197 [36 # 54]

W.L. Richards, "A Critique of a New Testament Text-Critical Methodology - The Claremont Profile Method", *JournBibLit* 96 (1977), 555-566 [22 # 704]

W.L. Richards, *The Classification of the Greek Manuscripts of the Johannine Epistles*, Missoula: Scholars Press, 1977 [22, p 337]

W.L. Richards, "Test Passages *or* Profiles: A Comparison of Two Text-Critical Methods", *JournBibLit* 115 (1996), 251-269 [41 # 85]

P.R. Rodgers, "The New Eclecticism. An essay in appreciation of the work of Professor George D. Kilpatrick", *NovTest* 34 (1992), 388-397 [37 # 615]

R.B. Stewart (ed), *The Reliability of the New Testament. Bart D. Ehrman & Daniel B. Wallace in Dialogue*, Minneapolis: Fortress, 2011 [55, p 567]

J.C. Thorpe, "Multivariate Statistical Analysis for Manuscript Classification", *TC: A Journal of Biblical Textual Criticism* 7 (2002) [47 # 1452]

S. Timpanaro, *The Genesis of Lachmann's Method*, Chicago & London: University of Chicago Press, 2005 [50, p 385]

K. Wachtel, "The Coherence Method and History", *TC: A Journal of Biblical Textual Criticism* 20 (2015)

D.B. Wallace, "The Text of the New Testament", *GraceTheolJourn* 9 (1988), 279-285 [33 # 1041r]

D.B. Wallace, "Challenges in New Testament Textual Criticism for the Twenty-First Century", *JournEvangTheolSoc* 52 (2009), 79-100 [53 # 1563]

D.B. Wallace (ed), *Revisiting the Corruption of the New Testament. Manuscript, Patristic, and Apocryphal Evidence*, Grand Rapids: Kregel, 2011 [56, p 389]

T. Wasserman, "The Coherence Based Genealogical Method as a Tool for Explaining Textual Changes in the Greek New Testament", *NovTest* 57 (2015), 206-218 [59 # 687]

T. Wasserman, "Historical and Philological Correlations and the CBGM as Applied to Mark 1:1", *TC: A Journal of Biblical Textual Criticism* 20 (2015)

R.D. Wettlaufer, *No Longer Written. The Use of Conjectural Emendation in the Restoration of the Text of the New Testament, the Epistle as a Case Study*, Leiden & Boston: Brill, 2013 [57, p 629]

Editions

R. Aasgaard, "Brothers in Brackets? A Plea for Rethinking the Use of [ ] in NA/UBS", *JournStudNT* 26 (2004), 301-321 [48 # 1540]

B. Aland et al, *Novum Testamentum Graecum. Editio Critica Maior*. Vol 4/1, *Catholic Letters: James*. Part 1, *Text*; part 2, *Supplementary Material*, Stuttgart: Deutsche Bibelgesellschaft, 1997 [43, p 175]

B. Aland, "*Novum Testamentum Graecum Editio Critica Maior*: Presentation of the First Part: The Letter of James", *TC: A Journal of Biblical Textual Criticism* 3 (1998)

B. Aland et al, *Novum Testamentum Graecum. Editio Critica Maior*. Vol 4/2, *Catholic Letters: The Letters of Peter*. Part 1, *Text*; part 2, *Supplementary Material*, Stuttgart: Deutsche Bibelgesellschaft, 2000 [45, p 172]

B. Aland et al, *Novum Testamentum Graecum. Editio Critica Maior*. Vol 4/3, *Catholic Letters: The First Letter of John*. Part 1, *Text*; part 2, *Supplementary Material*, Stuttgart: Deutsche Bibelgesellschaft, 2003 [48, p 425]

B. Aland et al, *Novum Testamentum Graecum. Editio Critica Maior*. Vol 4/4, *Catholic Letters: The Second and Third Letter of John, The Letter of Jude*. Part 1, *Text*; part 2, *Supplementary Material*, Stuttgart: Deutsche Bibelgesellschaft, 2005

K.D. Clarke, *Textual Optimism. A Critique of the United Bible Societies' Greek New Testament*, Sheffield: Sheffield University Press, 1997 [41, p 532]

K.D. Clarke, "Textual Certainty in the United Bible Societies' *Greek New Testament*", *NovTest* 44 (2002), 105-133 [46 # 1478]

B.D. Ehrman, "*Novum Testamentum Graecum Editio Critica Maior*: An Evaluation", *TC: A Journal of Biblical Textual Criticism* 3 (1998)

P.H. Davids, "*Novum Testamentum Graecum Editio Critica Maior*: A Non-Specialist's Perspective", *TC: A Journal of Biblical Textual Criticism* 3 (1998)

E.J. Epp, "The International Greek New Testament Project: Motivation and History", *NovTest* 39 (1997), 1-20 [41 # 1464]

P. Ellingworth, "The UBS *Greek New Testament*, Fourth Revised Edition: A User's Response", *NTStud* 42 (1996), 282-287 [40 # 1361]

J.K. Elliott, "The Third Edition of the United Bible Societies' Greek New Testament", *NovTest* 20 (1978), 242-277 [24 # 28r]

J.K. Elliott, "An Examination of the Twenty-sixth Edition of Nestle-Aland *Novum Testamentum Graece*", *JournTheolStud* 32 (1981), 19-49 [25 # 791]

J.K. Elliott, "The International Project to Establish a Critical Apparatus to Luke's Gospel", *NTStud* 29 (1983), 531-538 [28 # 437]

J.K. Elliott, "Why the International Greek New Testament Project is Necessary", *RestorQuart* 30 (1988), 195-206 [33 # 543]

J.K. Elliott, "A Comparison of Two Recent Greek New Testaments", *ExpTimes* 107 (1996), 105-106 [40 # 1362]

J.K. Elliott et al, "The *Marc Multilingue* Project", *FilolNT* 15 (2002), 3-17 [50 # 1672]

J.K. Elliott, "Manuscripts Cited by Stephanus", *NTStud* 55 (2009), 390-395 [54 # 85]

J.K. Elliott, "A New Edition of Nestle-Aland, *Greek New Testament*", *Journ TheolStud* 64 (2013), 47-65 [57 # 1538]

R.J. Goodrich, *A Reader's Greek New Testament*, 2nd edition, Grand Rapids: Zondervan, 2007 [54, p 145]

M.W. Holmes (ed), *The Greek New Testament. SBL Edition*, Atlanta: Society of Biblical Literature and Bellingham: Logos Bible Software, 2010 [55, p 362]

A.J. Forte, "Observations on the 28th Revised Edition of Nestle-Aland's Novum Testamentum Graece", *Biblica* 94 (2013), 268-292 [58 # 64]

P.M. Head, "*Editio Critica Maior*: An Introduction and Assessment", *TynBull* 61 (2010), 131-152 [55 # 91]

M. Holmes et al, The SBL Greek New Testament: Papers from the 2011 SBL Panel Review Session, *TC: A Journal of Biblical Textual Criticism* 17 (2012)

J.D. Karavidopoulos, "The Ecumenical Patriarchate's 1904 New Testament Edition and Future Perspectives", *SacScript* 10 (2012), 7-14 [57 # 76]

A. Merk (ed), *Novum Testamentum Graece et Latine apparatu critico instructum*, 11th edition, Rome: Editirice Pontificio Istituto Biblico, 1992 [39, p 496]

B.M. Metzger, "History of Editing the Greek New Testament", *Princeton SemBull* 8 (1987), 33-45 [32 # 47 & 526]

I.A. Moir, "Can We Risk Another 'Textus Receptus'?" *JournBibLit* 100 (1981), 614-618 [26 # 806]

Novum Testamentum Graece, 26th edition, Stuttgart: Deutsche Bibelgesell-schaft, 1979 [24, p 75]

Novum Testamentum Graece, 27th edition, Stuttgart: Deutsche Bibelgesell-schaft, 1993 [39, p 319]

Novum Testamentum Graece, 28th edition, Stuttgart: Deutsche Bibelgesell-schaft, 2012 [57, p 601]

D.C. Parker, "A Critique of the *Novum Testamentum Graecum Editio Critica Maior*", *TC: A Journal of Biblical Textual Criticism* 3 (1998)

W.L. Peterson, "Some Remarks on the First Volume (The Epistle of James) of the *Novum Testamentum Graecum Editio Critica Maior*", *TC: A Journal of Biblical Textual Criticism* 3 (1998)

E. Rummel, *Erasmus and His Catholic Critics*, vol 1, *1515-1522*, vol 2, *1523-1536*, Nieuwkoop: De Graaf, 1989 [34, p 379]

The Greek New Testament, 3rd corrected edition, New York: United Bible Societies, 1983 [28, p 193]

The Greek New Testament, 4th revised edition, New York: United Bible Societies, 1993 [39, p 314]

The UBS Greek New Testament. Reader's Edition with Textual Notes, Stuttgart: Deutsche Bibelgesellschaft, 2010 [55, p 368]

D. Trobisch, *A User's Guide to the Nestle-Aland 28 Greek New Testament*, Atlanta: Society of Biblical Literature, 2013 [58, p 384]

F. Voss & R. Omanson, "The Textual Base for Modern Translations of the New Testament", *RevExp* 108 (2011), 253-261 [56 # 830]

K. Wachtel, "Responses to Four Reviews of the James Volume of the *Editio Critica Maior*", *TC: A Journal of Biblical Textual Criticism* 3 (1998)

T.Wasserman, "Proposal for a New Rating System in Greek New Testament Editions", *BibTrans* 60 (2009), 140-157 [54 # 87]

B.F. Westcott & F.J.A. Hort, *The Greek New Testament*, Peabody: Hendrickson, 2007 [52, p 376]

Manuscripts

R.S. Bagnall, *Early Christian Books in Egypt*, Princeton & Oxford: Princeton University Press, 2009 [54, p 137]

D. Barker, "The Dating of New Testament Papyri", *NTStud* 57 (2011), 571-582 [56 # 825]

J. Bentley, *Secrets of Mount Sinai. The Story of the World's Oldest Bible - Codex Sinaiticus*, Garden City: Doubleday, 1986 [31, p 89]

J.N. Birdsall, "Two Lectionaries in Birmingham", *JournTheolStud* 35 (1984), 448-454 [29 # 463]

S.D. Charlesworth, "Public and Private – Second- and Third-Century Gospel Manuscripts", *Buried History* 42 (2006), 25-36 [51 # 1572]

S.D. Charlesworth, "T.C. Skeat, $\mathfrak{P}^{64+67}$ and $\mathfrak{P}^4$, and the Problem of Fibre Orientation in Codicological Reconstruction", *NTStud* 53 (2007), 582-604 [52 # 60]

C. Clivaz & J. Zumstein (ed), *Reading the New Testament Papyri in Context. Lire les papyrus du Nouveau Testament dans leur contexte*, Leaven & Walpole: Peeters, 2011 [56, p 150]

P.W. Comfort, *Early Manuscripts & Modern Translations of the New Testament*, Wheaton: Tyndale, 1990 [35, p 91]

P.W. Comfort, "Exploring the Common Identification of Three New Testament Manuscripts: $\mathfrak{P}^4$, $\mathfrak{P}^{64}$ and $\mathfrak{P}^{67}$", *TynBull* 46 (1995), 43-54 [40 # 64]

P.W. Comfort, "New Reconstructions and Identifications of New Testament Papyri", *NovTest* 41 (1999), 214-230 [44 # 56]

P.W. Comfort & D.P. Barrett (ed), *The Text of the Earliest New Testament Greek Manuscripts*, Wheaton: Tyndale, 2001; corrected and enlarged edition of *The Complete Text of the Earliest New Testament Manuscripts*, Grand Rapids: Baker, 1999 [43, p 569]

J.K. Elliott, *Codex Sinaiticus and the Simonides Affair. An Examination of the nineteenth century claim that Codex Sinaiticus was not an ancient manuscript*, Thessaloniki: Patriarchal Institute for Patristic Studies, 1982 [28, p 305]

J.K. Elliott, *A Survey of Manuscripts Used in Editions of the Greek New Testament*, Leiden & New York: Brill, 1987 [32, p 232]

J.K. Elliott, *A Bibliography of Greek New Testament Manuscripts*, Cambridge & New York: Cambridge University Press, 1989 [33, p 377]

J.K. Elliott, "Biblical Manuscripts in Manchester", *ExpTimes* 110 (1998), 50-51 [43 # 826]

J.K. Elliott, "Five New Papyri of the New Testament", *NovTest* 41 (1999), 209-213 [44 # 57]

J.K. Elliott, "The Biblical Manuscripts of the John Rylands University Library of Manchester", *BullJohnRylUnivLibMan* 81 (1999), 3-50 [45 # 73]

J.K. Elliott, "Seven Recently Published New Testament Fragments from Oxyrhynchus", *NovTest* 42 (2000), 209-213 [45 # 74]

J.K. Elliott, *A Bibliography of Greek New Testament Manuscripts*, Cambridge: Cambridge University Press, 2000 [45, p 146]

J.K. Elliott with J.N. Birdsall, "Supplement to J.K. Elliott, *A Bibliography of Greek New Testament Manuscripts*", *NovTest* 46 (2004), 376-400 [49 # 824]

J.K. Elliott, "Supplement II to J.K. Elliott, *A Bibliography of Greek New Testament Manuscripts*", *NovTest* 49 (2007), 370-401 [52 # 827]

J.K. Elliott, "Supplement III to J.K. Elliott, *A Bibliography of Greek New Testament Manuscripts*", *NovTest* 52 (2010), 272-297 [55 # 90]

I.M. Ellis, "Codex Bezae and Recent Enquiry", *IrBibStud* 4 (1982), 82-100 [27 # 37]

C.A. Evans, "How Long Were Late Antique Books in Use? Possible Implications for New Testament Textual Criticism", *BullBibRes* 25 (2015), 23-37 [59 # 682]

H. Förster, "7Q5 = Mark 6.52-53: A Challenge for Textual Criticism?", *Journal of Greco-Roman Christianity and Judaism* 2 (2001-05), 27-35 [50 # 1685]

P. Foster, "Variant Readings of New Testament Greek Manuscripts", *ExpTimes* 122 (2011), 335-337 [55 # 1550]

P.M. Head, "The Date of the Magdalen Papyrus of Matthew (*P.Magd.Gr.* 17 = P64): A Response to C.P. Thiede", *TynBull* 46 (1995), 251-285 [40 # 1364]

P.M. Head, "Some Recently Published NT Papyri from Oxyrhynchus: An Overview and Preliminary Assessment", *TynBull* 51 (2000), 1-16 [45 # 75]

P.M. Head, "Fragments of Six Newly Identified Greek Bible Manuscripts in a Cambridge Collection: A Preliminary Report", *TC: A Journal of Biblical Textual Criticism* 8 (2003)

P.M. Head, "Is $\mathfrak{P}^4$, $\mathfrak{P}^{64}$ and $\mathfrak{P}^{67}$ the Oldest Manuscript of the Four Gospels? A Response to T.C. Skeat", *NTStud* 51 (2005), 450-457 [50 # 126]

P.M. Head, "P. Bodmer II ($\mathfrak{P}^{66}$): Three Fragments Identified", *NovTest* 47 (2005), 105-108 [50 # 260]

P.M. Head, "The Gospel of Mark in Codex Sinaiticus: Textual and Reception-Historical Considerations", *TC: A Journal of Biblical Textual Criticism* 13 (2008)

P.M. Head, "Five New Testament Manuscripts: Recently Discovered Fragments in a Private Collection in Cambridge", *JournTheolStud* 59 (2008), 520-545 [53 # 812]

J.R. Howell, "The Characterization of Jesus in Codex W", *JournEarlyChrist Stud* 14 (2006), 47-75 [50 # 1567]

L.W. Hurtado, "The Origin of the *Nomina Sacra*: A Proposal", *JournBibLit* 117 (1998), 655-673 [43 # 827]

L.W. Hurtado (ed), *The Freer Biblical Manuscripts. Fresh Studies of an American Treasure Trove*, Atlanta: Society of Biblical Literature, 2006 [51, p 371]

D. Jongkind, *Scribal Habits of Codex Sinaiticus*, Piscataway: Gorgias, 2007 [51, p 556]

Y.K. Kim, "Palaeographical Dating of $\mathfrak{P}^{46}$ to the Later First Century", *Biblica* 69 (1988), 248-257 [33 # 57]

J. Krans, "Codex Boreelianus (F 09) and the IGNTP Edition of John", *TC: A Journal of Biblical Textual Criticism* 15 (2010)

T.J. Kraus & T. Nicklas (ed), *New Testament Manuscripts. Their Texts and Their World*, Leiden & Boston: Brill, 2006 [51, p 153]

D. Lafleur, "Which Criteria for Family 13 (f13) Manuscripts?", *NovTest* 54 (2012), 105-148 [56 # 1582]

A. Luijendijk, "A New Testament Papyrus and Its Documentary Context: An Early Christian Writing Exercise from the Archive of Leonides (*P.Oxy.* II 209/$\mathfrak{P}^{10}$)", *JournBibLit* 129 (2010), 575-596 [55 # 825]

S. McKendrick, *In a Monastery Library. Preserving Codex Sinaiticus and the Greek Written Heritage*, London: British Library, 2007 [51, p 557]

S. McKendrick & K. Doyle (ed), *Bible Manuscripts. 1400 Years of Scribes and Scripture*, London: British Library, 2007 [52, p 151]

P. Malik, "The Earliest Corrections in Codex Sinaiticus: Further Evidence from the Apocalypse", *TC: A Journal of Biblical Textual Criticism* 20 (2015)

P. Mayerson, "Codex Sinaiticus: An Historical Observation", *BibArch* 46 (1983), 54-56 [27 # 860]

B.M. Metzger, *Manuscripts of the Greek Bible. An Introduction to Greek Palaeography*, New York & Oxford: Oxford University Press, 1981 [26, p 76]

B.M. Metzger, "Two manuscripts of the Greek gospels in Cape Town", *Neotestamentica* 20 (1986), 59-60 [31 # 519]

J.E. Miller, "Some Observations on the Text-Critical Function of the Umlauts in Vaticanus, with Special Attention to 1 Corinthians 14.34-35", *JournStudNT* 26 (2003), 217-236 [48 # 809]

M.M. Mitchell & P.A. Duncan, "Chicago's 'Archaic Mark' (MS 2427): a Reintroduction to Its Enigmas and a Fresh Collation of Its Readings", *NovTest* 48 (2006), 1-35 [50 # 989]

I.A. Moir, "Tischendorf and the Codex Sinaiticus", *NTStud* 23 (1976), 108-115 [21 # 322]

A.Q. Morton, "A Gospel Made to Measure", *Journal of Higher Criticism* 12 (2006), 63-67 [51 # 1574]

B. Nongbri, "The Use and Abuse of $\mathfrak{P}^{52}$: Papyrological Pitfalls in the Dating of the Fourth Gospel", *HarvTheolRev* 98 (2005), 23-48 [50 # 267]

J.C. O'Neill, "The Rules Followed by the Editors of the Text Found in the Codex Vaticanus", *NTStud* 35 (1989), 219-228 [33 # 1048]

P. Orsini & W. Clarysse, "Early New Testament Manuscripts and Their Dates. A Critique of Theological Palaeography", *EphTheol Lov* 88 (2012), 443-474 [57 # 1540]

D.C. Parker, *Codex Bezae. An early Christian manuscript and its text*, Cambridge & New York: Cambridge University Press, 1992 [36, p 415]

D.C. Parker, "Was Matthew Written before 50 CE? The Magdalen Papyrus of Matthew", *ExpTimes* 107 (1995), 40-43 [40 # 718]

D.C. Parker, "Greek Gospel Manuscripts in Bucharest and Sofia", *BullJohn RylUnivLibMan* 85 (2003), 3-12 [51 # 1575]

D.C. Parker, *Codex Sinaiticus. The Story of the World's Oldest Bible*, London: British Library and Peabody: Hendrickson, 2010 [55, p 364]

D.C. Parker & C.-B. Amphoux (ed), *Codex Bezae. Studies from the Lunel Colloquium, June 1994*, London, New York, Cologne: Brill, 1996 [41, p 138]

D.C. Parker & M.B. Morrill, "Some New Manuscripts of the Greek New Testament in Boston and Cambridge", *HarvTheolRev* 95 (2002), 237-244 [46 # 1480]

D. Parker & J.N. Birdsall, "The Date of the Codex Zacynthius (Ξ): A New Proposal", *JournTheolStud* 55 (2004), 117-131 [48 # 1543]

P.B. Payne, "The Text-Critical Function of the Umlauts in Vaticanus with Special Attention to 1 Corinthians 14.34-35: A Response to J. Edward Miller", *JournStudNT* 27 (2004), 105-112 [49 # 51]

P.B. Payne & P. Canart, "The Originality of Text-Critical Symbols in Codex Vaticanus", *NovTest* 42 (2000), 105-113 [44 # 1561]

S.E. Porter & W.J. Porter (ed), *New Testament Greek Papyri and Parchments. New Editions*, Berlin & New York: de Gruyter, 2008 [55, p 365]

G.E. Rice, "Is Bezae a Homogeneous Codex?" *PerspRelStud* 11 (1984), 39-54 [29 # 865]

C.H. Roberts & T.C. Skeat, *The Birth of the Codex*, New York & London: Oxford University Press, 1983 [28, p 308]

J.M. Robinson, *The Story of the Bodmer Papyri. From the First Monastery's Library in Upper Egypt to Geneva and Dublin*, Eugene: Cascade, 2011 [55, p 367]

S. Siikavirta, "𝔓²⁷ (Papyrus Oxyrhynchus 1355): A Fresh Analysis", *TC: A Journal of Biblical Textual Criticism* 18 (2013)

T.C. Skeat, "The Codex Vaticanus in the Fifteenth Century", *JournTheolStud* 35 (1984), 454-465 [29 # 466]

T.C. Skeat, "The Codex Sinaiticus, the Codex Vaticanus, and Constantine", *JournStudNT* 50 (1999), 583-625 [44 # 803]

R.B. Stone, "The Life and Hard Times of Ephraemi Rescriptus", *BibToday* 24 (1986), 112-118 [30 # 976]

R.J. Swanson (ed), *New Testament Greek Manuscripts. Variant Readings Arranged in Horizontal Lines against Codex Vaticanus: Matthew*, Sheffield: Sheffield Academic Press, 1995 [40, p 527]

R.J. Swanson (ed), *New Testament Greek Manuscripts. Variant Readings Arranged in Horizontal Lines against Codex Vaticanus: Mark; Luke; John*, Sheffield: Sheffield Academic Press, 1995 [41, p 153]

R.J. Swanson (ed), *New Testament Greek Manuscripts. Variant Readings Arranged in Horizontal Lines against Codex Vaticanus: The Acts of the Apostles*, Sheffield: Sheffield Academic Press, 1998 [43, p 593]

R.J. Swanson (ed), *New Testament Greek Manuscripts. Variant Readings Arranged in Horizontal Lines against Codex Vaticanus: Galatians*, Wheaton: Tyndale, 1999 [44, p 403]

R.J. Swanson (ed), *New Testament Greek Manuscripts. Variant Readings Arranged in Horizontal Lines against Codex Vaticanus: Romans*, Wheaton: Tyndale, 2001 [46, p 388]

R.J. Swanson (ed), *New Testament Greek Manuscripts. Variant Readings Arranged in Horizontal Lines against Codex Vaticanus: 1 Corinthians*, Wheaton: Tyndale, 2003 [50, p 421]

R.J. Swanson (ed), *New Testament Greek Manuscripts. Variant Readings Arranged in Horizontal Lines against Codex Vaticanus: 2 Corinthians*, Wheaton: Tyndale, 2005 [50, p 421]

C.P. Thiede, "Greek Qumran Fragment 7Q5: Possibilities and Impossibilities", *Biblica* 75 (1994), 394-398 [39 # 684]

C.P. Thiede, "Notes on 𝔓⁴ = Bibliotheque Nationale Paris, Supplementum graece 1120/5", *TynBull* 46 (1995), 55-57 [40 # 67]

C.P. Thiede, "Papyrus Magdalen Greek 17 (Gregory-Aland 𝔓⁶⁴): A Reappraisal" *TynBull* 46 (1995), 29-42 [40 # 68]

C.P. Thiede, "7Q5 - Facts or Fiction?" *WestTheolJourn* 57 (1995), 471-474 [40 # 720]

C.P. Thiede, "The Magdalen Papyrus. A Reply", *ExpTimes* 107 (1996), 240-241 [41 # 86]

C.M. Tuckett, *"Nomina Sacra* in Codex E", *JournTheolStud* 57 (2006), 487-499 [51 # 838]

J.W. Voelz, "The Greek of Codex Vaticanus in the Second Gospel and Marcan Greek", *NovTest* 47 (2005), 209-249 [50 # 202]

D.B. Wallace, "7Q5: The Earliest NT Papyrus?" *WestTheolJourn* 56 (1994), 173-180 [39 # 38r]

T. Wasserman, "Papyrus 72 and the *Bodmer Miscellaneous Codex*", *NTStud* 51 (2005), 137-154 [49 # 1566]

T. Wasserman, "Some Bibliographic Notes on Greek New Testament Manuscripts", *NovTest* 49 (2007), 291-295 [52 # 61]

T. Wasserman, "A Comparative Textual Analysis of $\mathfrak{P}^4$ and $\mathfrak{P}^{64+67}$", *TC: A Journal of Biblical Textual Criticism* 15 (2010)

Scribal habits

P. Comfort, "Scribes as Readers: Looking at New Testament Textual Variants according to Reader Reception Analysis", *Neotestamentica* 38 (2004), 28-53 [49 # 1562]

P.M. Head, "Observations on Early Papyri of the Synoptic Gospels, especially on the 'Scribal Habits'", *Biblica* 71 (1990), 240-247 [36 # 613]

P.M. Head, "Christology and Textual Transmission: Reverential Alterations in the Synoptic Gospels", *NovTest* 35 (1993), 105-129 [38 # 46]

J. Hernández, *Scribal Habits and Theological Influences in the Apocalypse. The Singular Readings of Sinaiticus, Alexandrinus, and Ephraemi*, Tübingen: Mohr Siebeck, 2006 [51, p 400]

J. Hernández et al, "Scribal Habits in Early Greek New Testament Papyri: Papers from the 2008 SBL Panel Review Session", *TC: A Journal of Biblical Textual Criticism* 17 (2012)

W.C. Kannaday, "'Are Your *Intentions* Honorable?': Apologetic Interests and the Scribal Revision of Jesus in the Canonical Gospels", *TC: A Journal of Biblical Textual Criticism* 11 (2006)

E.A. Nida, "The 'harder reading' in textual criticism: an application of the second law of thermodynamics", *BibTrans* 32 (1981), 101-107 [25 # 794]

J.M. Ross, "The 'Harder Reading' in Textual Criticism", *BibTrans* 33 (1982), 138-139 [26 # 808]

J.R. Royse, "The Treatment of Scribal Leaps in Metzger's *Textual Commentary*", *NTStud* 29 (1983), 539-551 [28 # 439]

J.R. Royse, *Scribal Habits in Early Greek New Testament Papyri*, Leiden: Brill, 2008 [52, p 575]

Patristics

J.A. Brooks, *The New Testament Text of Gregory of Nyssa*, Atlanta: Scholars Press, 1991 [36, p 101]

G. Donker, "Athanasius's Contribution to the Alexandrian Textual Tradition of the Pauline Epistles: An Initial Exploration", *TC: A Journal of Biblical Textual Criticism* 13 (2008)

G.J. Donker, *The Text of the Apostolos in Athanasius of Alexandria*, Atlanta: Society of Biblical Literature, 2011 [56, p 152]

B.D. Ehrman, G.D. Fee, M.W. Holmes, *The Text of the Fourth Gospel in the Writings of Origen*, vol 1, Atlanta: Scholars Press, 1992 [37, p 276]

G.D. Fee, "The Text of John and Mark in the Writings of Chrysostom", *NTStud* 26 (1980), 525-547 [25 # 28]

G.D. Fee, "Origen's Text of the New Testament and the Text of Egypt", *NTStud* 28 (1982), 348-364 [27 # 38]

D.D. Hannah, *The Text of 1 Corinthians in the Writings of Origen*, Atlanta: Scholars Press, 1997 [41, p 556]

J. Hernández, "The Relevance of Andrew of Caesarea for New Testament Textual Criticism", *JournBibLit* 130 (2011), 183-196 [55 # 1551]

R.L. Mullen, *The New Testament Text of Cyril of Jerusalem*, Atlanta: Scholars Press, 1997 [41, p 539]

C.D. Osburn, "The Text of the Pauline Epistles in Hippolytus of Rome", *SecondCent* 2 (1982), 97-124 [27 # 40]

C.D. Osburn, "Methodology in Identifying Patristic Citations in NT Textual Criticism", *NovTest* 47 (2005), 313-343 [50 # 837]

G. Quispel, "Marcion and the Text of the New Testament", *VigChrist* 52 (1998), 349-360 [43 # 830]

Majority Text

G.H. Clark, *Logical Criticisms of Textual Criticism*, 2nd edition, Jefferson: Trinity Foundation, 1990 [35, p 230]

G.D. Fee, "Modern Textual Criticism and the Revival of the *Textus Receptus*", *JournEvangTheol Soc* 21 (1978), 19-33 [22 # 702]

G.D. Fee, "A Critique of W.N. Pickering's *The Identity of the New Testament Text*. A Review Article", *WestTheolJourn* 41 (1979), 397-423 [24 # 365r]

Z.C. Hodges, "Modern Textual Criticism and the Majority Text: A Response", *JournEvangTheol Soc* 21 (1978), 143-155 [23 # 38]

Z.C. Hodges & A.L. Farstad (ed), *The Greek New Testament according to the Majority Text*, Nashville: Nelson, 1982 [27, p 201]

M.W. Holmes, "The 'Majority text debate': new form of an old issue", *Themelios* 8 (1983), 13-19 [27 # 859]

J. Krans, "Erasmus and the Text of Revelation 22:19: A Critique of Thomas Holland's *Crowned With Glory*", *TC: A Journal of Biblical Textual Criticism* 16 (2011)

T.P. Letis (ed), *The Majority Text: Essays and Reviews in the Continuing Debate*, Fort Wayne: Institute for Biblical Textual Studies, 1987 [32, p 235]

W.N. Pickering, *The Identity of the New Testament Text*, Nashville & New York: Nelson, 1977 [22, p 84]

W.N. Pickering, "Queen Anne ... ' and All That: A Response", *Journ EvangTheolSoc* 21 (1978), 165-167 [23 # 41]

T.J. Ralston, "The 'Majority Text' and Byzantine Origins", *NTStud* 38 (1992), 122-137 [36 # 1134]

M.A. Robinson, "New Testament Textual Criticism: The Case for Byzantine Priority", *TC: A Journal of Biblical Textual Criticism* 6 (2001) [47 # 1449]

M.A. Robinson, "Crossing Boundaries in New Testament Textual Criticism: Historical Revisionism and the Case of Frederick Henry Ambrose Scrivener", *TC: A Journal of Biblical Textual Criticism* 7 (2002) [47 # 1448]

M.A. Robinson & W.G. Pierpont, *The New Testament in the Original Greek According to the Byzantine/Majority Textform*, Atlanta: Original Word Publishers, 1991 [36, p 257]

M.A. Robinson & W.G. Pierpont, *The New Testament in the Original Greek: Byzantine Textform 2005*, Southborough: Chilton, 2005. With an appendix "The Case for Byzantine Priority".

H.P. Scanlon, "The Majority Text Debate: Recent Developments", *BibTrans* 36 (1985), 136-140 [29 # 866]

H.A. Sturz, *The Byzantine Text-Type and New Testament Textual Criticism*, Nashville: Nelson, 1984 [29, p 201]

R.A. Taylor, "Queen Anne Resurrected? A Review Article", *JournEvang TheolSoc* 20 (1977), 377-381 [22 # 342r]

J. van Bruggen, *The Ancient Text of the New Testament*, Winnipeg: Premier Printing, 1976 [21, p 81]

D.B. Wallace, "Some Second Thoughts on the Majority Text", *BiblSac* 146 (1989), 270-290 [34 # 56]

D.B. Wallace, "The Majority Text and the Original Text: Are They Identical?", *BiblSac* 148 (1991), 151-169 [35 # 1065]

D.B. Wallace, "Inspiration, Preservation, and New Testament Textual Criticism", *GraceTheol Journ* 12 (1991), 21-50 [37 # 616]

D.B. Wallace, "The Majority-Text Theory: History, Methods and Critique", *JournEvangTheolSoc* 37 (1994), 185-215 [39 # 685]

D.B. Wallace, "Historical Revisionism and the Majority Text Theory: The Cases of F.H.A. Scrivener and Herman C. Hoskier", *NTStud* 41 (1995), 280-285 [39 # 1348]

Theological implications

J.A. Borland, "Re-examining New Testament Textual-Critical Principles and Practices Used to Negate Inerrancy", *JournEvangTheol Soc* 25 (1982), 499-506 [28 # 38]

K.W. Clark, "The Theological Relevance of Textual Variation in Current Criticism of the Greek New Testament", *JournBibLit* 85 (1966), 15

P. Ellingworth, "Text, Translation, and Theology. The New Testament in the Original Greek?" *FilolNT* 13 (2000), 61-73 [47 # 758]

E.J. Epp, "The Multivalence of the Term 'Original Text' in New Testament Textual Criticism", *HarTheolRev* 92 (1999), 264-65 [44 # 58]

W.C. Kannaday, "'Are Your *Intentions* Honorable?': Apologetic Interests and the Scribal Revision of Jesus in the Canonical Gospels", *TC: A Journal of Biblical Textual Criticism* 11 (2006)

J. Sexton, "NT Text Criticism and Inerrancy", *MastSemJourn* 17 (2006), 51-59 [51 # 71]

G. Simpson, "Inspiration and the Text of the New Testament", *UBS Journal* 2.1 (2004), 16-22

Miscellaneous

J. Delobel, "The Achilles' Heel of New Testament Textual Criticism", *Bijdragen* 63 (2002), 3-21 [47 # 76]

B.D. Ehrman, "Text and Tradition: The Role of New Testament Manuscripts in Early Christian Studies. Part 1: Text and Interpretation: The Exegetical Significance of the 'Original' Text", Part 2: Text and Transmission: The Historical Significance of the 'Altered' Text", *TC: A Journal of Biblical Textual Criticism* 5 (2000) [47 # 1445]

D.C. Parker, Review of Metzger and Ehrman, *Journal of Theological Studies* 57 (2006), 551-567 [51 # 836r]

J.M. Ross, "Some Unnoticed Points in the Text of the New Testament", *NovTest* 25 (1983), 59-72 [27 # 862]

J.M. Ross, "Floating Words: Their Significance for Textual Criticism", *NTStud* 38 (1992), 153-156 [36 # 1135]

J.M. Ross, "Further Unnoticed Points in the Text of the New Testament", *NovTest* 45 (2003), 209-221 [48 # 77]

H. Szesnat, "'Some Witnesses Have ... ': The Representation of the New Testament Text in English Bible Versions", *TC: A Journal of Biblical Textual Criticism* 12 (2007)

www.ingramcontent.com/pod-product-compliance
Lightning Source LLC
Chambersburg PA
CBHW022008090426
42741CB00007B/942